The Fourth Guardsman

James Franklin "Bud" Ledbetter

(1852–1937)

by
Glenn Shirley

EAKIN PRESS ★ Austin, Texas

FIRST EDITION

Copyright © 1997
By Glenn Shirley

Published in the United States of America
By Eakin Press
An Imprint of Sunbelt Media, Inc.
P.O. Drawer 90159   ★   Austin, TX 78709-0159

9   8   7   6   5   4   3   2

ISBN 1-57168-172-8 HB

ISBN 1-57168-566-9 PB

Contents

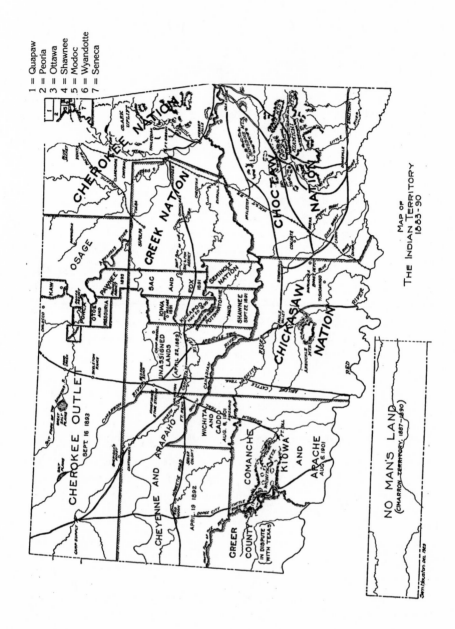

MAP OF
THE INDIAN TERRITORY
1865-90

1 = Quapaw
2 = Peoria
3 = Ottawa
4 = Shawnee
5 = Modoc
6 = Wyandotte
7 = Seneca

iv

Preface

Indians, homesteaders, and politicians made Oklahoma the wonder state of the nation, but it was the pioneer lawmen who paved the way to peace and its greatness. Under the handicaps of insufficient compensation and assistance, these men risked their lives daily to rout the criminal hordes that plagued the Twin Territories.

From the close of the Civil War past the turn of the century, the lands of the Five Civilized Tribes—roughly the eastern half of Oklahoma, known as Indian Territory or "The Nations"—consisted of a volcanic society. Murder, rape, robbery, whiskey peddling and stock thievery peaked during the 1890s. Into this miasma of crime a rough giant of a man strode by virtue of his incredible judgment and sheer bravery, wearing a badge of deputy United States marshal and wielding a Colt's revolver and a Winchester rifle with which he could shoot the lobe off a man's ear and never put a mark on his jaw.

His name was James Franklin Ledbetter.

Ledbetter's service spanned the dissolution of the Indian tribes, the culmination of the shifting federal court jurisdiction over Indian Territory, and the decade following the advent of the Twin Territories as the forty-sixth state of the Union. He stood staunchly for law and order, was honored repeatedly by outstanding law enforcement officials and the electorate alike, and won the distinction of having engaged in more than 100 battles with criminals and never being scratched. A household expression of the time was: "When Ledbetter comes after you, you better go!"

In private life, he was gentle, courteous, and unassuming. In the autumn of his life, he became affectionately known as "Uncle Bud." He had very little to say about the events of his career and never bothered to confirm or deny many of the stories told about him. Some of the stories undoubtedly exist only in the minds of old-timers. However, more than enough can be documented to distinguish him as the "Fourth Guardsman" alongside Bill Tilghman, Heck Thomas, and Chris Madsen—the triumvirate of manhunters famed as the "Three Guardsmen" of Oklahoma.

This is the Ledbetter saga.

GLENN SHIRLEY
Stillwater, Oklahoma
1997

Chapter 1

Ax-Handle Justice

ARKANSAS NUMBERS James Franklin Ledbetter among her famous native sons. He was born December 15, 1852, in a log cabin on War Eagle Creek in the Boston Mountains, six miles south of Huntsville, Madison County. The county was named for President James Madison, and Huntsville was an old place, established as the county seat in 1839. A log courthouse thirty feet square was built that year; a brick seat of justice came into use in 1845; and the town was incorporated in 1852, less than a month prior to Ledbetter's birth.

His parents were moderately well-to-do farm folk whose ancestors emigrated from England. Since his father's name was also James Franklin, he was first called "Little Jimmy." When he was seven, the family moved farther west to a place on Drake's Creek. There Little Jimmy alternately attended public school, did farm chores, and became adept at hewing building logs and fence rails with saw and ax. In his spare time, he roamed the loblolly pine and hardwood forests, where game was plentiful and the streams abounded with fish. He became an expert with rod and rifle, and greatly supplemented the family larder.

Living in the backwoods, the Ledbetters suffered little from the Civil War. Federal troops burned the Huntsville courthouse in 1863, and the Masonic Hall was used as the seat of justice until 1871, when a new courthouse was erected.

1

Little Jimmy became a strapping, broad-shouldered six-feet-two, ruddy faced, and, in the vogue of the era, nurtured an adolescent mustache that soon grew thick and stylish. He had a scent keener than a bird dog. His taciturn demeanor and level, blue-eyed gaze marked him as a man not to be trifled with. His nickname was no longer considered appropriate, so he was given a second one, "Turk." But somehow that didn't seem to fit, so folks called him "Bud," which stuck the rest of his life.

Bud's parents died in 1871, and he assumed the responsibilities of the family farm. Life became humdrum the next two years, and he might have succumbed to the call of adventure had he not become enamored of a Boston Mountain girl. At age twenty-two, on June 24, 1874, he married Mary Josephine Terry in a Madison County church. A son, George W., was born to the couple August 28, 1875, followed in 1877 by a daughter named America Jane "Dolly."

Meanwhile, Madison County was given new vigor. A branch of the St. Louis and San Francisco railroad was built from Fayetteville into the county's southern section. West to east along this route, several lumber camps and rural trading points thrived—Thompson, Delaney, Powell, Combs, Saint Paul.

There was more activity, however, in Johnson County adjoining southeast. The St. Louis, Iron Mountain, and Southern railroad between Fort Smith and Little Rock ran through the lumbering and rich coal area around Clarksville. The county's alluvial bottom lands, drained by numerous creeks and the Arkansas River, were excellent for raising cotton, corn, and grasses. Its sandy clay uplands were among the best in the state for growing peaches, grapes, berries, and garden products. Bud saw a greater market for agricultural and horticultural products in the flouring, planing, and roller mills and cotton shipping towns along the railroad's river route. In 1879 he moved his family near the new boomtown of Coal Hill, fourteen miles west of Clarksville.[1]

Coal Hill was the center of the coal region worked by Pennsylvania miners. One summer afternoon Bud drove into the boisterous settlement for supplies. While waiting for his order he decided to "have a look around," and though strictly a teetotaler, he casually strolled into one of the many saloons.

On this occasion of his first visit to Coal Hill, Bud was wearing a white linen suit, and the unusual garb attracted the several roughly dressed miners and mill hands gathered inside. Their sense of judgment dulled by raw whiskey, they failed to take into account the stature of the stranger. Immediately they surrounded him, fingering and tugging at his suit "to test the material." One tough jerked Bud's shirttail from his pants to "see if it was real silk."

Bud's eyes chilled. Without a word he walked out of the place, followed by jeers from the group. He went down the street to a hardware store and purchased a hefty new oaken ax handle. He then returned to the saloon and closed and locked the door behind him.

Some passersby heard a commotion inside. Unable to gain entrance, they hastily summoned the town mayor. This official, with the help of several citizens, forced open the door and saw half a dozen saloon habitués scattered on the pine floor, unconscious. Bud leaned on the bar, tapping the heavy ax handle across the palm of his big left hand, his gaze boring into the mayor, and asking: "What are you going to do about it?"

The mayor, momentarily disconcerted, didn't reply. Finally he turned to the crowd, and said: "Clear these bums out of here, then we'll get to the bottom of this."

Getting to the bottom of the affair amounted to the town fathers insisting that Bud accept the job of marshal. They had long searched for one in vain. It was a call Bud couldn't resist.

He was as appalled as Coal Hill's responsible citizens by the dangerous conditions. The town was a fertile place for gunplay. Bud had plenty of experience with a rifle from his hunting days in the Boston Mountains, and could smash a whiskey glass on a post at twenty paces with a six-shooter simply by pointing the weapon. In most cases, however, he had only to "club" the violator off to confinement. It was a language the miners understood and respected.

"I didn't have to kill anybody," Bud recalled in later years, "but I skinned a few of 'em up pretty bad before I got the whip hand."

At the same time he launched a campaign against the vice-ridden drinking establishments and sin-dens. Acting on legal warrants and injunctions, he padlocked the joints one by one. Still, he was a fair and reasonable man. These hot spots provided what miners considered wholesome recreation, and joints agreeing to strict supervision were allowed to reopen.

"Soon it was safe for decent womenfolk to walk down the street without being insulted or molested," Bud said, "and a peace loving fellow could step into a saloon for a drink without being messed up or rawhided."[2]

His enforcement methods caught the attention of some of Arkansas' best known peace officers. Sheriff E. T. McConnell, the square-jawed, hard-fisted disciple of law and order at Clarksville, rode over to Coal Hill.

"Anybody who can put a lid on this town is a born lawman," he told Bud. "I can use a fellow like you as a deputy."

The proposal surprised Bud. "I don't know," he said. "I'm satisfied here."

"Satisfied enough to turn down double the pay you are getting now?" asked McConnell.

Bud wasn't *that* satisfied. He became deputy sheriff of Johnson County, "a position he filled for fourteen years, discharging his duties with marked promptness and fidelity." Under the tutorship of his partner, veteran Deputy Sheriff John Powers, he soon learned to ferret the criminal from his lair or track him down, and whetted his endowed abilities of observation and retention. Together, he and Powers became known to the thieves and killers of the sections as "The Invincibles."[3]

Chapter 2

Deputy Sheriff of
Johnson County

SHORTLY AFTER PINNING on the deputy's badge, Bud established a reputation for "dogged pursuit." The fugitive in question was a dapper-looking, black-mustached Johnson County native named James T. Holland.

Holland had killed a man for $100. A woman who witnessed the killing and saw Holland dividing the loot with a friend was later poisoned, allegedly by Holland. Bud arrested Holland and jailed him at Clarksville, charging him with both crimes. The dual murders aroused the entire community, which enabled Holland's attorney to obtain a change of venue to Ozark, seat of adjoining Franklin County. The attorney's "smooth talk" failed to impress the Ozark jury; Holland was found guilty and sentenced to hang.[1]

The drama did not end there, however. Some of Holland's friends anticipated the outcome of the case, and while the verdict was being read they allegedly were bribing the local jailer. After the sentence was pronounced and Holland was returned to his cell, the jailer conveniently left the door unlocked, allowing Holland to escape. Horses and guns were waiting behind the jail, and the convicts were well on their way when the break was reported.

One of the escapees was a boy from Blantons, Bedford

County, Tennessee, who had come to work at Ozark. He soon became homesick, and having no money for railroad fare, stole a horse from his employer, which he sold in Johnson County. He had "transacted his deal in fine shape until he went to buy a ticket." Then Bud "stepped up and arrested him."

The boy and Holland had become good friends in the Ozark jail. During the trial, the boy had proposed to Holland that, if allowed to escape as had been planned, they would go their separate ways and meet at his father's farm near Blantons, where Holland could hide out until the hunt cooled. Accordingly, Holland avoided his Johnson County haunts and headed straight for the boy's home.

Sheriff McConnell sent Ledbetter after the killer, and for the next twenty-eight days and nights, Bud trailed him out of Arkansas, across Mississippi into northwestern Alabama, thence northward into Bedford County, Tennessee—a distance of 1,000 miles, on horseback! Often Bud would be only a day behind the fugitive. But within 100 miles of Blantons, Holland traded for a fresh horse and supplies, and managed to elude his pursuer. After several days without a clue to the man's where-abouts, Bud gave up the trail in disgust. Before returning to Arkansas, he furnished Sheriff Hammon of Bedford County and the sheriffs of all adjoining counties a full description of Holland, telling them he was wanted—dead or alive.

Meanwhile, the boy horse thief reached home in good time. He told his people of his trouble in Arkansas, but made no men-tion of Holland, or that he, too, would be arriving soon. His old father told him to hide in the hills until "the thing blew over." The boy complied, seeing no one, and his people not mention-ing that he had been home.

Holland arrived at the farm a few days later, informing the father that he had helped his son escape jail and that his son had promised he could hide there for a time. Knowing nothing about Holland and deciding from his dapper appearance and the pistol he carried that he was a detective looking for his boy, the old man told him that he hadn't seen his son, but he had to go into town for supplies and Holland could feed his horse in the barn and rest until he returned.

The old man went to Shellyville, instead of Blantons, and

informed Sheriff Hammon of the stranger's presence. The stranger fit the description Hammon had received from Ledbetter, and the sheriff planned with the old man to ride to the farm after dark, slip up to the house while the family was at supper, and hopefully make the capture without incident.

Sheriff Hammon reached the farm at dusk and hid in the timber until suppertime. The old man seated Holland with his back to the front door. After the family began eating, the sheriff quietly stepped in and ordered: "Hands up!" Holland offered no resistance. He was jailed at Shellyville, waived extradition, and Hammon telegraphed Ledbetter that he would start to Clarksville with his man at once.

Word spread that the killer would arrive on a certain train. While Bud was waiting at the station to relieve the sheriff of the prisoner, a friend warned him that a mob was waiting outside Clarksville to take Holland off the train and lynch him. Bud intercepted Hammon by telegraph at a way station east of Clarksville. The sheriff took Holland off the train and went cross-country to Ozark, on horseback.

The friend's warning proved correct. As the train neared Clarksville, the engineer sighted a pile of railroad ties on the track. He braked to a stop just as the engine pushed into the barricade, and was surrounded by an armed mob ordering him to "stay put." Several of the men rushed back to the coaches, telling the conductor it was not a holdup—they only wanted a certain passenger who was in custody of the Tennessee sheriff. The conductor told them that no such parties were on the train. Not believing him, they searched every coach and finally removed the ties from the track. As the train started moving again, the conductor called out: "Boys, you were too near home. The sheriff took your man off at the last station back." The leader replied: "We'll get the son-of-a-bitch before morning." And the mob started for Ozark.

Meanwhile, Hammon and Ledbetter lodged Holland in the Ozark jail. The Tennessee sheriff entrained for home, and Bud departed for Clarksville. The Franklin County sheriff, in charge of the jail keys, was confident all was quiet for the night, so he went home and to bed. About 2:30 in the morning, he was called from his house on the pretext that a man he wanted had been captured, and was confronted by half a dozen masked men armed with six-shooters and rifles. They took his keys, two of the men guarded him, and the others went to the jail. They dragged Holland from his cell, hanged him from a tree in the jailyard, and pumped a dozen bullets into his writhing body at point-blank range. Then the mob dissolved into the night.[2]

Bud learned of the episode and vowed to arrest any man he found to have been involved. He did not believe in vigilante action, and regardless of the crimes committed, felt that Holland should have been legally hanged as the Ozark judge and jury had edicted. Sheriff McConnell did not encourage any arrests, however, and most people in Johnson County considered that justice had been done.

Bud starred again in 1883 following an attempted robbery of the St. Louis, San Francisco, and Southern railway train near Mulberry, Franklin County, thirty miles west of Clarksville. On March 7, four young men nonchalantly boarded the train when it stopped at Mulberry and took seats in a passenger coach. Being "ordinary looking fellows," they attracted little attention from the other passengers. As the train moved westward, they pulled large bandannas from their pockets. Still they were paid no heed—until conductor John Cain entered the coach, punching tickets, and was confronted by the masked quartet.

"We ain't got no tickets," one of the youths leered, whipping a revolver from his waistband. "This is a holdup!"

As the astonished conductor reached for the emergency cord, the youth thumbed a quick shot. Cain collapsed in the aisle of the coach, a bullet in his chest.

Brakeman Lester heard the shot and entered the coach to investigate. A second bullet from the youth's revolver creased his head and sent him spinning to the floor. Shouting and screaming passengers dived behind the seats. The other bandits began firing. Leaden slugs shattered the glass from a couple of windows, splintered the woodwork, and knocked the pipe from the iron stove in the forepart of the coach, filling the air with soot and smoke. The bandits' plan, whatever it was, suddenly went awry. They tangled with each other in the narrow aisle, and in the melee shot one of their own in the side and a leg. They then bolted into the vestibule of the coach, and with wild abandon, flung themselves from the moving train.

Brakeman Lester managed to jerk the emergency cord and bring the train to a jolting stop. Except for minor cuts from the flying fragments of glass and wood splinters, the passengers were not injured. Conductor Cain was bleeding badly, and it was decided to back the train to Mulberry to secure the quickest medical attention. The engineer opened the throttle, moving the train too fast on the reverse run for boarding when it passed the spot where the bandits jumped off, but saw no sign of them along the track. At Mulberry, Cain died, and a posse departed from the robbery site at once.

The news reached Clarksville by telegraph, and Sheriff McConnell sent his two "Invincibles" to assist the Franklin County authorities. Ledbetter and Powers boarded the next westbound train. With them was a young posseman named Paden Tolbert.

Paden was the son of J. R. Tolbert, a newspaperman and an orchardist from Georgia, who had built his home on an acreage north of Clarksville and had established the *Johnson County Herald* in 1878. J. R. spiced his editorials on the possibilities of growing Georgia peaches in Johnson County as avidly as he supported Sheriff McConnell's views on law enforcement. Paden had been educated in Georgia and taught school for a time, but preferred a life out of doors. He was an apt pupil of Sheriff McConnell, proficient with a Winchester and Colt's six-shooter, a boon companion of Ledbetter, and volunteered for posse duty at every opportunity. It was J. R.'s premonition that, sooner or later, his son would give up teaching and peach-growing for law enforcement as a profession.

Ledbetter, Powers, and Tolbert reached the holdup scene within an hour. The Mulberry posse had found the wounded bandit hiding in a heavy thicket along the track. In no condition to ride, his companions had abandoned him. Despite being left behind, he refused to reveal their identities.

Bud soon located the spot where the bandits had staked their horses before going into Mulberry to board the train. The trail of the remaining three bandits led northward toward the densely timbered mountains above Arkansas. While Powers sent word to Sheriff McConnell that an extensive hunt appeared in the offing, Bud rented a mule and loaded it with supplies, including several boxes of ammunition. The fact that the bandits had boarded the train unmasked branded them as amateurs, but with a murder charge in addition to attempted robbery hanging over their heads, they likely would be a difficult and dangerous trio to corner.

For three weeks, whenever possible, Paden Tolbert furnished his father accounts of the manhunt, and the *Johnson County Herald* kept Clarksville citizens advised of the progress of Ledbetter and Powers. The trail zig-zagged over the mountain ridges, doubled back and crossed and recrossed itself so often that ordinary lawmen might have given up the chase. But not the "Invincibles." They finally sighted their quarry, and the ragged, weary fugitives surrendered without a fight. When brought into Ozark to be jailed with their captured companion, one of the bandits, nearly exhausted, grumbled to the crowd that gathered: "Them bastards would've followed us to hell, if necessary."

All four youths were local characters—brothers "Gov" and Jim Johnson, Jim Herndon, and Monroe McDonald. They were charged in Franklin County, but the public defender succeeded in obtaining a change of venue to Clarksville. This seemed a mistake—the Holland case was still fresh in the memories of Johnson County people. The four were found guilty and sentenced to be hanged on June 22, 1883, at Clarksville, for the murder of Cain.

The small gallows at the courthouse could not accommodate four men efficiently, so Sheriff McConnell had a special gibbet erected on an open lot near the railroad depot. A few days prior to the execution, McConnell was one of the speakers at the state convention of Arkansas sheriffs in Little Rock. In his concluding remarks, he noted that he would shortly hang four murderers and would-be train robbers, and received such a round of applause that he invited the entire body of officers to come to Clarksville to see how law was enforced in his county. Forty-two sheriffs were present when the condemned men fell through the trap.[3]

McConnell was a very busy man. Aside from being sheriff, he owned a drug store and several farms, and welcomed the opportunity to give up his office in 1885 when W. S. Jett, a prominent Clarksville citizen, agreed to run for sheriff. Jett shared McConnell's views, possessed the same iron drive, and with McConnell's endorsement and support of the *Johnson County Herald,* he easily won election. Ledbetter and Powers stayed on as deputies, and Jett added Paden Tolbert as a full-time deputy on October 7. Five years later, Powers succeeded Jett as sheriff, and continued the law enforcement policies of both Jett and McConnell.

Johnson County's era of violence waned, and Paden Tolbert, ever restless, looked to the law enforcement possibilities in Indian Territory where crime was at its peak. The numerous hangings edicted by Judge Isaac C. Parker at Fort Smith and the recent establishment of the United States court districts in the Nations simply meant, to Paden, that more was to come.

In the summer of 1891, he ended his tenure as an Arkansas deputy and became a deputy marshal for the federal court at Muskogee. He was stationed in the Cherokee Nation, and moved his family to Vinita.

Ledbetter continued his service under Sheriff Powers. But the glowing accounts of adventures that Tolbert sent to Clarksville promised longed-for excitement. Early in 1894, Bud decided to explore for himself the law enforcement opportunities beyond the Arkansas border.

Chapter 3

Indian Territory:
"Hotbed of Crime"

THE 64,000 SQUARE MILES between Arkansas and the Texas pan-
handle, excluding the Neutral Strip, or No Man's Land, was
known as the Twin Territories. Oklahoma Territory, roughly
the western half, consisted of lands opened to the homestead
settlement by the "runs" of 1889, 1891, 1892, and 1893, with the
Osage, Kickapoo and far southwestern Indian reservations attached for judicial purposes. Indian Territory, roughly the eastern half, consisted of the lands of the Five Civilized Tribes and
seven small bands of Indians occupying the Quapaw Agency at
the extreme northeastern corner of the Cherokee Nation.

Some 60,000 Cherokee, Creek, Choctaw, Chickasaw, and
Seminole full bloods and mixed bloods, 4,000 intermarried
whites, and 19,000 "freedmen" (Negro slaves of the Indians
emancipated after the Civil War and adopted into the tribes with
full rights of citizenship) occupied approximately 31,000 square
miles to which Indian Territory was confined. In addition, more
than 400,000 outlanders had drifted into the area. Most were
employees of railroads and related operations under the federal government's classification of "traders." Every business and
profession was represented in the Indian towns that had
boomed as commercial centers. Ranchers leased grazing rights.

Farmers rented Indian lands for one-third of the crops raised. Included, of course, were their families.

Thousands were there, however, without government or tribal permits, many of them fugitives from justice or lawless persons attracted to the Territory by its freedom from legal restraints. Though the Indians called for the removal of these "intruders," the government hardly found it possible or feasible. With the Indians so sadly in the minority and half a million whites being denied the right to hold land or have any voice in the Indian governments, even to the extent of providing schools for their children, a movement already had begun to abolish the tribal organizations and bring the Twin Territories into the Union as a single state.

Each tribe, except the Seminole (who operated under an organic law), had a governor or principal chief as executive officers, cabinet officers, and a national council or legislative body to enact laws for their people. District judges and a supreme court adjudicated civil and criminal matters. District sheriffs and their deputies enforced the Indian statutes and preserved the peace, aided by a national force of mounted police called the "lighthorsemen." There were local constables, town marshals, and policemen as well. Many of the Indian officers carried deputy U.S. marshal commissions. They assisted the federal deputies in dealing with the prohibited manufacture, sale, and use of liquor, and helped hunt down horse and cattle thieves and the robber gangs that made Indian Territory, according to the border press, "a hotbed of crime."

Three major railroads traversed the Territory—the Missouri, Kansas, and Texas (Katy) from Chetopa, Kansas, through Vinita, Wagoner, Muskogee, and South McAlester to Denison, Texas; the Atlantic and Pacific from southwestern Missouri through Vinita, thence westward as the St. Louis and San Francisco (Frisco) through Claremore, Red Fork and Sapulpa, toward Oklahoma Territory; and the St. Louis, Iron Mountain and Southern (Arkansas Valley route) from Coffeyville, Kansas, through Claremore, Wagoner and Sallisaw to Fort Smith. These railroads employed detectives and guards to protect passengers and the valuable express matter they transported.

So there were opportunities galore for an experienced lawman like Ledbetter.

Bud stopped briefly at Fort Smith, where he was offered a deputy's commission under Col. George J. Crump, United States marshal for the Western District of Arkansas. Crump was a Confederate Army veteran who had served three years after the war as clerk of Carroll County, adjoining Madison. He had been admitted to the bar in 1869, and practiced law at Carrollton, then at Harrison, in Boone County, before being appointed marshal by President Grover Cleveland in 1893. He remembered Bud's growing-up years in Madison County and had heard much of his exploits as deputy sheriff at Clarksville.

Crump needed men like Ledbetter, not only to protect the fundamental rights and freedoms of the Indian and white citizen within Judge Parker's jurisdiction, but to serve federal writs, efficiently. And he told Ledbetter so. Bud, however, was anxious to see Paden Tolbert again, and to first look around the new federal districts of Indian Territory.

The volume of work in Judge Parker's court had increased tremendously by the late 1880s. The distance and difficulty of reaching the Fort Smith seat of justice with criminal violators was so great that prosecutions were avoided when possible, and it was almost as great a hardship to be summoned to Fort Smith as a witness. Tribal authorities had long objected to their citizens being dragged to an adjoining state for trial before juries composed of residents outside the Territory. Of equal concern was the lack of jurisdiction in civil cases involving white noncitizens and those who had left the states and taken up abode in the Nations to avoid creditors.[1]

All of which Congress found unsatisfactory, and by act of March 1, 1889, had established the first "white man's court" in the Territory at Muskogee, Creek Nation, putting in force the laws of Arkansas to adjudicate civil cases, if the amount involved exceeded $100. Though principally for civil purposes, the Muskogee court was also given exclusive, original jurisdiction of all offenses committed in the Territory not punishable by death or imprisonment at hard labor—in no way interfering, however, with the criminal jurisdiction of the court at Fort Smith. In addition, the act provided for a district judge, prosecuting attorney, and U.S. marshal to be appointed by the president for a term of four years.[2]

By act of May 2, 1890, which created the Oklahoma Territory with an independent judicial system, Congress had extended the laws of Arkansas relating to practice, pleadings, and procedure to Indian Territory and divided the jurisdiction of the Muskogee court, due to the volume of work, into three divisions—the first, embracing the Cherokee and Creek nations and Quapaw Agency, with headquarters at Muskogee; the second, the Choctaw Nation, with headquarters at South McAlester; the third, the Seminole and Chickasaw nations, with headquarters at Ardmore. Each division was given a separate judge, prosecuting attorney and U.S. marshal, three U.S. commissioners with the powers of justices of the peace under the laws of Arkansas, and conferred *concurrent* jurisdiction with the Fort Smith court on federal offenses committed in Indian Territory. Indian courts were allowed to retain exclusive jurisdiction of all civil and criminal cases in which only members of the tribes were involved. Further, the district judges were given the same power as the governor of Arkansas to extradite persons taking refuge in Indian Territory, charged with crimes in the states and other territories of the United States, and to sue requisitions upon governors of states and other territories for persons who had committed offenses in Indian Territory and taken refuge in such states and territories.[3]

During the one-year period between the passage of these two acts, 110 killings, more or less wilful and premeditated, had been committed in the Indian nations. No state or territory in the Union had furnished one-half as many homicides, population compared, thus stigmatizing Indian Territory a more bloodthirsty land than any other commonwealth.

Since 1890, organized bands of bank and train robbers had swept the Territory, raiding across its borders into Kansas, Texas, Arkansas, and Missouri. Only two of the more notorious gangs had run afoul of the law—the Daltons, who had met disaster at Coffeyville in 1892, and the Henry Starr band, broken up in 1893. Starr himself still languished in the Fort Smith jail pending an appeal to the U.S. Supreme Court after being twice sentenced to hang for murdering one of Crump's deputies.

"These courts out there have been swamped with stock thievery and weapon assault cases, and brush-skulking whiskey peddlers, who take their life in one hand and their six-shooter in the other, are as thick as flies," Crump told Ledbetter. "Why, in one week during its last [January] term, the South McAlester court disposed of 120 such cases." Seventy-three deputies and possemen had been killed or wounded by the officers while resisting or fleeing from arrest.[4]

This was not the glowing picture of conditions Paden Tolbert had painted in his letters to Clarksville. But Ledbetter was not perturbed.

"That's why I need good men," Crump reiterated.

Bud nodded. He thanked the marshal for his consideration, and entrained for Vinita.

Chapter 4

A Murder Avenged

THE LEDBETTER-TOLBERT reunion was a memorable affair. Paden lost no time acquainting Bud with his many friends— men who had ridden in his posses, town officials, businessmen, and particularly small, gray-haired H. E. "Sam" Ridenhour, a former deputy for the Fort Smith court and presently chief of Vinita's fire department. Ridenhour had come to the area in 1872. For hours, he regaled Bud with stories of how Vinita was spawned where the Atlantic and Pacific railroad crossed the Katy railroad and why many old-timers still called it "The Junction."

A Katy survey crew that struck camp on the high prairie south of Cabin Creek in the fall of 1869 were under instructions to locate a station thirty miles south of the Kansas border as a first stop on the railroad's proposed route through Indian Territory and the Gulf. Their record of chain lengths told them they had reached that point, and the magnificent country adjacent the circumambulent line of timber north and east, following Cabin Creek southward toward the Neosho (Grand) River, convinced them that no finer location could be found for a future thriving town. By late May 1871, the iron rails had pushed to the delta of the creek and a bridge spanned the stream.

The survey of the Atlantic and Pacific, by mutual agreement, was to cross the Katy at this point, and everything ran smoothly until its roadbed was completed within a mile and a half to the east.

"Then," Ridenhour said, "all hell broke loose."

Col. E.C. Boudinot, noted Cherokee lawyer and diplomat who had spent much time in Washington, fenced a two-square-mile area where the Old Military Road split with the Texas cattle trail and bore northeastward. Boudinot then arranged with the Atlantic and Pacific to abandon the old survey and cross the Katy at this more elevated prairie site, hoping to own the entire town. Without warning, between two suns, the Atlantic and Pacific came with camps, baggage, and a wagon loaded with a huge iron railroad crossing, which they placed over the Katy track. Disgusted and with armed resistance, the Katy people tore up the crossing and stood guard day and night, slowly dragging trains back and forth to prevent the Atlantic and Pacific making headway. Nearly five months elapsed before an injunction was granted and the Atlantic and Pacific crossed the Katy three miles to the north.

The new site was surveyed and platted and named Downingville, in honor of Lewis Downing, chief of the Cherokee Nation. Boudinot's fencing was torn down and destroyed, but he succeeded in having the town renamed Vinita, in honor of the noted sculptress Lavinia "Vinnie" Ream, whom he had known and allegedly romanced while in Washington. Thus "The Junction" became the new trading center for the northern part of the Cherokee Nation.

The town began as a scattering of tents and board shanties, occupied mostly by toughs and whiskey peddlers. Brawls and fights were frequent. Men were killed. During the 1880s, Vinita passed another turbulent period as a shipping point for the vast herds of Texas longhorns that roamed the unsettled prairies and were marketed in Kansas City and St. Louis. The town marshal had his hands full, and the city fathers sent for L. P. Isbell, a deputy for the Fort Smith court stationed at Fort Gibson. Isbell calmed the rough element, and since the arrival of Paden Tolbert, Vinita had been a more peaceable place to live. It was headquarters for one of the three U.S. commissioners in the Muskogee division. Deputy marshals from Muskogee came there for arraignment of violators arrested in the region, and on other federal business. And that, Ridenhour believed, explained why Vinita had escaped the depredations of the outlaw gangs roving Indian Territory.

Ledbetter toured the town and liked what he saw— scores of substantial frame houses; blocks of well-stocked retail stores and other businesses, including two hotels to accommodate the many who stopped off the railroads; a bank established in 1892; a post office; a federal jail; and a courthouse in the offing. Four weekly newspapers, started in the 1870s primarily for political purposes, were failing, but the *Indian Chieftain,* started in 1882, was enjoying continuous publication. Wagons, buggies, and surreys daily lined the extra wide and permanently marked streets.

Bud also liked the people. Full-bloods, but mostly three-fourth and half-blood Cherokees, carried on the major part of the business. White men in business were married to Indian women, which permitted them to operate in their own names. And there was the usual quota of physicians, lawyers, and other professionals. The town supported the Worcester Academy, a public school for Indian students. The Congregationalist, Methodist, and Presbyterian churches made available their facilities for the education of white children.[1]

Bud broached the possibility of moving his family to Vinita and riding for the federal court at Muskogee. Tolbert and Ridenhour agreed on the educational and cultural aspects of life in Vinita, but felt that obtaining a deputy's commission at Muskogee was out of the question.

The turnover of federal officials in the western territories had been rife ever since Grover Cleveland's inauguration for his second term as president. In the Muskogee division of Indian Territory, he had appointed Charles B. Stuart, of Gainesville, Texas, to succeed James M. Shackleford as judge; Clifford L. Jackson, of Muskogee, to succeed Z. T. Walrond as district attorney; and James J. McAlester, of South McAlester, to succeed Thomas N. Needles as United States marshal.

McAlester was a native of Sebastian County, Arkansas, and had been a captain in the Confederate Army. After the war, he had freighted and worked for post traders from Fort Smith to Fort Sill, married into a prominent Indian family, and in 1870 discovered the best outcroppings of coal in the Choctaw Nation.

The Katy railroad needed quality coal to fuel its engines, and upon completion of the railway line past McAlester's store and trading post, his mining operations flourished as the Choctaw Nation's leading industry. McAlester had leased his mining company to an operating coal company, from which he received a royalty, and erected a two-story home of cypress planks shipped from the southeastern United States, with light fixtures imported from Belgium, which had become the setting for entertainment of prominent guests all over the country. He lacked law enforcement experience, but his business ability and familiarity with Indian Territory impressed President Cleveland.

In accepting the Muskogee appointment, McAlester had announced that he would upgrade the office with the finest quality of deputies, but had retained a few of Needles' men. Tolbert was among those to go, but his federal service had not been interrupted. He had remained at Vinita as a Fort Smith deputy, appointed by U.S. Marshal Crump in May 1893. Tolbert considered McAlester an "aggressive opportunist," the "coal king" of the town that bore his name. His only affinity for the new marshal was the fact that he had been born in Arkansas.

"It's all politics at Muskogee," Ridenhour added.

Bud had never played the politics game—never worried about supporting the wrong horse during his years as deputy sheriff in Arkansas. Close-mouthed, even with the men he worked with, and so adroit at eliciting information he desired without persons being aware they had divulged anything, he had always gone all out in whatever he undertook, which usually resulted in getting his man. To him, experience and character were what counted. But he wasn't too proud to accept whatever work was available, so long as it was in the law enforcement field.

Stealing cattle for sale or slaughter was a big threat in northeastern Indian Territory. The Cherokee Stockmen's Protective and Detective Association had been organized in 1884 to assist the cattlemen in putting an end to the rustling. Ridenhour was a close friend of the association's president, and he offered to recommend Bud as a stock detective.

Tolbert suggested that Bud might find guarding the Katy line through the Territory more profitable and attractive. Katy trains had been derailed, held up, and looted regularly during the reign of the Dalton and Starr outlaws. Copy-cat gangs were on the rise. The newly organized William Tuttle "Bill" Cook and Crawford "Cherokee Bill" Goldsby band of marauders had killed the station agent in Nowata in an attack on the Arkansas Valley railroad, July 5, 1894, and ten days later, held up the Frisco train at Red Fork, in the Creek Nation. The railroads faced the problem of having enough reliable guards over money and packages sent by express. Deputy marshals often guarded the express cars. Tolbert himself frequently rode the Katy line. The duty, though dangerous, provided extra income.

This was the excitement Bud was looking for; he signed as a guard for the American Express Company operating in conjunction with the Katy system. His run was to be from Chetopa, Kansas, through Vinita, Adair, Pryor Creek, Wagoner, and Muskogee to Checotah, Creek Nation—and return. He moved his family to Vinita and disposed of his interests in Arkansas.

En route from Coal Hill in mid-July, Bud stopped in Fort Smith to advise Marshal Crump of his decision and to visit briefly with a chum of his Madison County days, Tom Isom. Tolbert had agreed to accompany Bud on his first run for the American Express. On July 25, Bud telegraphed that he had been detained at Fort Smith for "killing a tough man who was under bond for killing Officer Wiley Cox."[2]

Cox was a native of Clarksville, who had come to Fort Smith in 1873, entered public service, and achieved a reputation as "an excellent officer, a first-class detective." In October 1890, he had been shot during an altercation with Joe McNally, "a peaceable citizen when sober, but when drinking a dangerous man." Cox had struggled with his wound "until blood poisoning set in and he died April 13, 1891."[3]

The assault charge against McNally had been upgraded to murder. Yet after three years of legal maneuvering, he remained free on bail, his case untried in the Sebastian County courts.

About 11:00 Monday night, July 23, Bud, obsequious to his friend Isom, who was in his cups, accompanied Isom to Doc Rogers' saloon, where Isom and a man named Gardenhier renewed an old difference and came to blows. The Fort Smith

Elevator of July 27 reported the subsequent events: "Ledbetter interposed and endeavored to suppress the row." Joe McNally, who was with Gardenhier and also under the influence, "drew his pistol and either intentionally or accidentally discharged it, the bullet passing near Ledbetter and striking the opposite wall. . . . Officer John Fuller arrived on the scene a few moments later, and induced McNally to give up his gun." A man named Bullock agreed to walk McNally and Gardenhier home. Ledbetter and another friend of Isom's, named Morrow, took Isom home. Fuller, "supposing the trouble was all over, went home and to bed."

Meanwhile, McNally and Gardenhier were "stopping at the Keating saloon, corner of Third and the Avenue." Bullock objected to their entering, and McNally "drew a revolver, cocked it and punched him in the stomach. Where he secured this revolver no one seems to know." Leaving Gardenhier at Keating's, McNally took Bullock back to Doc Rogers' saloon and resumed his drinking.

After putting Isom to bed, Morrow felt the need for a "nightcap," and Bud, supposing that McNally had gone home, returned with Morrow to Rogers' saloon. It was now 11:30 P.M.

As Bud and Morrow entered, "McNally drew his gun and pulled down on Ledbetter. The latter slowly backed to the side door, keeping his eye on McNally. As Ledbetter stepped down on the stone coping, both men fired simultaneously. McNally's shot went wide and imbedded itself in a door on the opposite side of the alley. Ledbetter's aim was true, the bullet striking McNally in the right breast, passing through his body and plowing into a door just behind him. The mortally wounded man staggered and fell, never uttering a word. In less than five minutes he was dead."

After the shooting, Bud went to Marshal Crump's office and "remained there until morning, where he surrendered to Chief Deputy Sheriff R. M. Fry, of Sebastian County." At the preliminary examination Tuesday afternoon, Bud was represented by attorneys Judge Blythe and James Brizzolara. "From the testimony adduced, Squire Kennedy dismissed the action against Ledbetter, and he was released."

The Vinita *Indian Chieftain* of July 26 briefed the affair without comment. The *Muskogee Phoenix* of August 2 suggested that Bud's record as deputy sheriff in Johnson County "played an important role" in the inquisition. The Tahlequah *Cherokee Advocate* of August 1 called Bud "a good man, a splendid officer," adding: "We need such men in the Territory, and we have them, too."

McNally was buried in Oak Cemetery at Fort Smith, Wednesday afternoon, July 25. In a sense, the murder of Wiley Cox had been avenged.

Chapter 5

Train Robbery at Blackstone Switch . . .

A FEW DAYS AFTER KILLING McNally, Ledbetter boarded the Katy train in Kansas on his first trip for the American Express. Tolbert joined him at Vinita. A large sum of money was being moved from a Kansas City bank to a bank in Fort Worth, and the express company anticipated an attack by the Cook-Cherokee Bill gang. The gang, however, was robbing the Lincoln County Bank at Chandler, Oklahoma Territory, and the money shipment went through without incident.

In the robbery at Chandler, a citizen was killed and one of the outlaws, Elmer "Chicken" Lucas, wounded and captured. On August 2, a posse of deputy marshals and Euchee Indian scouts engaged the fleeing bandits west of Sapulpa, where members Lon Gordon and Henry Munson were slain and Curtis Dayson was captured. During September and October, separate contingents of the gang led by Cook and Cherokee Bill raided a store at Okmulgee, the Arkansas Valley railway depots at Claremore and Fort Gibson, the Katy depot at Chouteau, and wrecked and robbed the Katy train at Coretta, south of Wagoner. After additional robberies in the Creek and Seminole nations, the Cook contingent fled into Texas, where Thurman "Skeeter" Baldwin, Jess Snyder, William Farris, and a cohort named Turner were captured in a battle with Texas Rangers in

Clay County. Cook escaped, but was apprehended a few weeks later in New Mexico, returned to Fort Smith and sentenced to forty-five years in the Albany, New York, prison. During Cook's flight to New Mexico, Cherokee Bill and his contingent robbed the store and post office at Lenapah, murdering an innocent bystander, Ernest Melton. This outrage, followed by the robbery of the Arkansas Valley depot at Nowata, general stores at Fort Gibson and Checotah, and the attempted robbery of a store at Braggs Station south of Fort Gibson, led to the killing of gang members Jim French, George Sanders, and Sam "Verdigris Kid" McWilliams, and the capture and eventual hanging of Cherokee Bill at Fort Smith.*

Strangely, the Cook–Cherokee Bill marauders had spared the Katy trains guarded by Tolbert and Ledbetter. Bud made several runs during these four months, and complained about his job being dull. But Express company officials told him to stay on. Something would happen when least expected.

The train crews constantly discussed what they would do in a holdup. Bud asked Katy engineer Joseph Hotchkiss what he would do if bandits boarded his cab and ordered him to stop. Hotchkiss replied: "Why, I'd just knock 'em in the head with my hammer and keep the train moving along."[1] But Hotchkiss forgot his boast and hammer completely the moonbright night of November 13, 1894, when the northbound Katy Flyer, carrying a shipment of $60,000 from Dallas, crossed the Arkansas River north of Muskogee and was attacked near Wybark, at Blackstone Switch.

Some writers have credited the attack to Bill Cook and his contingent, though they had been out of the Territory for almost three weeks. In fact, the success of the Cook–Cherokee Bill marauders had emboldened lesser jackals of the area, and the motley crew who struck the Katy Flyer consisted of Nathaniel "Texas Jack" Reed, a white man, small of stature, with keen, crafty eyes; Thomas "Tom" Root, a bad Cherokee of some

---

* The depredations of the Cook–Cherokee Bill gang are fully described in Glenn Shirley, *Marauders of the Indian Nations; The Bill Cook Gang and Cherokee Bill* (Barbed Wire Press, Stillwater, Oklahoma, 1994).

African–American blood; Buz Luckey, a hulking mulatto; and Will Smith, a black man. Luckey and Smith were believed to have been among Cook's cadre at the Coretta robbery of October 20.

Texas Jack was no criminal small fry. He was born in Madison County, Arkansas, in 1862, but never knew Ledbetter, who was ten years his senior, though they had been reared only eighteen miles apart. Of his early life, Reed said:

> My father, Mason H. Reed, a Union soldier, was killed in action on November 14, 1863, leaving my mother with two sons to support. Later, she married a man who was kind to me until her death in 1875. Then my stepfather married a Dutch widow with thirteen children, and I was shunted about among my relatives with no permanent home. I grew up without much education . . . left Madison County at age twenty-one . . . went to Kansas to work as a cowboy . . . but fell in with bad companions and took up banditry as a profession.[2]

He listed his major jobs from 1886 to 1892 in this order: A bank at Harper, Kansas; bank at Riverside, Texas; express at Brownsville, Texas; stage at Canyon Gap, Colorado; train at Phoenix, Arizona; train at El Paso, Texas; and a stage near San Antonio, where he had a "hard fight" with Rangers and won his appellation, Texas Jack.

> After San Antonio, I rode with the Dalton boys . . . was holding their horses at Coffeyville . . . so got away. I was with Bill Doolin in the fight with U.S. marshals at Ingalls [Oklahoma Territory] in 1893, and with Doolin in the bank robbery at Southwest City, Missouri [May 10, 1894].[3]

His affiliations with the Dalton and Doolin gangs were pure fabrication. Official records and contemporary reports do not bear him out. But it was a storyteller's prerogative.

Reed claimed that in the summer of 1894, while hibernating in an abandoned cabin on the farm of James "Jim" Dyer, a well-to-do white man living ten miles west of Wagoner, he was introduced to Smith, Root, and Buz Luckey. He would swear later that Dyer was the "brains" of the outfit; that Dyer had been informed by a contact in Dallas of the big money shipment on the Katy, "and the four of us besides Dyer made our plans."[4]

What Texas Jack hadn't been told was that Ledbetter, Tolbert, and posseman Sid Johnson were guarding the express coach strongbox.

Blackstone Switch was a long siding which ran into the bottoms between the Arkansas and Verdigris rivers to stock pens used for shipping cattle. The pens were so far off the main line that the siding resembled more of a spur than a sidetrack. Timber and thick underbrush secluded the pens from the main line. It was an ideal spot to hold up a train, and only a short ride from the Dyer farm.

According to Texas Jack, he, Dyer, Root, Smith, and Luckey viewed the location and rehearsed what each should do. Jack's duty was to cut the lock off the switch and send the train to the left onto the siding, then dynamite the express car if they were refused entrance. After the robbery, they were to meet at Vann's Ford on the Verdigris and divide the loot. At dark on November 13, all rendezvoused at the siding, except Dyer. At first, they thought he was just late. But as the 10:00 train time neared, Dyer had not put in an appearance, so the four decided to proceed as planned. As the train approached, Jack cut the lock and threw the switch . . .

The Katy Flyer was made up of the express and baggage car, a smoker, two passenger coaches, and a sleeper. Engineer Hotchkiss realized what was happening the moment the light changed from green to red. He set his brake, opened the sand valve, and brought the train to a screeching halt on the sidetrack as the sleeper reached the switch. He pulled the whistle four times, the prearranged signal to the guards that a holdup was about to take place. Then, "the brave engineer, who was going to crack them in the head with his hammer, jumped from the train, made for the open prairie, and hid in an arroyo."[5] The reason he gave for his action afterward was his fear of capture by the bandits and being compelled to assist in forcing entrance to the express car— usual train robbing procedure.

Hotchkiss had stopped the train sooner than the bandits who were further down the track expected. His dash into the arroyo infuriated them, and they came running toward the express, shooting and yelling, "Open up!" The messenger refused, and they poured a salvo into the wooden side of the car.

Miraculously, no occupant was hit. Ledbetter, his icy blue eyes snapping, his dark brown mustache bristling, and 220 pounds of hard muscle tensed for action, ordered the large side door thrown half open. Then he, Tolbert, and Johnson began throwing lead as fast as they could lever their Winchesters, and drove the bandits back. Texas Jack, in turn, hurled a bundle of explosives beneath the sill of the car. The guards saw it in time to duck to safety. The charge splintered the unopened section of the door, blew a hole in the floor, and ripped the platform off the end of the car, leaving it open to the bandits.

"Throw down your guns and come out reaching for the stars!" they shouted. The guards replied with a "withering blast" from the torn door and shattered end of the car. "The bandits had plenty of nerve, too, and instead of running, returned the fire." The fight continued nearly half an hour, "the bandits threatening to dynamite the rest of the train. But Bud and his men stuck to their posts and kept pumping their rifles." The fight "got so hot" that the bandits "decided it would be better not to push that part of the robbery any further," and changed tactics. Texas Jack donned a false chin beard made from the end of a cow's tail, tucked a grain sack under one arm, and while his cohorts engaged in a "sniping match," he slipped under the cover of some crossties stacked along the sidetrack "to pluck what daisies he could in the smoker."[6]

According to Texas Jack:

> I sprang onto the platform with my six-shooters in my hands, opened the door, and said, "Good evening, gentlemen." I asked them all to lock their hands over their heads and rise to their feet, which they did. "Now, gentlemen, fold your arms and sit down and don't move until you are asked to." I then handed the sack to a young man who sat near and asked him to oblige by collecting the contributions from the left side of the aisle. He took the sack promptly, for he could see I meant business. A man to my right straightened in his seat and said, "I am a reporter for the *St. Louis Globe Democrat.*" I said, "Then you are just the man to collect the contributions from the right side of the aisle." He refused. I pointed a gun at him and

never seen a man spring into the aisle quicker'n he did. I now had two helpers relieving the traveling public of their super- fluous wealth . . . .

They carried the sack through the entire train, and as we entered each coach, I shouted: "Everybody drop in your valu- ables, or be killed!"[7]

The conductor locked himself in the ladies closet, and enough curious things happened among the passengers to fill a chapter. Suffice it to say that, when Jack reached the end of the train, his sack contained "$460, eight gold and silver watches, and three pistols. . . . The fact that more loot was not secured was owing to the passengers hiding many of their valuables while the robbers were endeavoring to get into the express car."[8]

All went well for Texas Jack until he left the last coach and "started back to help give the express car another round." Led- better glimpsed him through a ragged aperture at the end of the car. "It was all Bud needed to crack down on him." The bul- let struck Jack in the upper left hip and ranged downward, cut- ting his bladder and lower bowels, and emerged from his right thigh. "I fired back," Jack said, "but in my upset state I was not accurate. . . ." He was able to drag himself and the sack of loot to the shelter of the crossties, "not allowing Ledbetter to get another shot." Buz Luckey, the big mulatto, ran to him, picked him up bodily, and carried him into the underbrush to his horse. After pouring another volley into the express and pas- senger coaches, Root and Smith rushed to their mounts, and the four bandits disappeared in the timber.[9]

Assured that the shooting was over, engineer Hotchkiss came out of hiding, backed the train onto the main line, and proceeded to Gibson Station on the Verdigris to await orders. "The train was detained something over an hour. . . . It looked as though it has been through a hail storm of lead."[10]

Texas Jack gave this account of the gang's escape:

We rode about a quarter of a mile, when nature called. The boys helped me down, and I drained freely. I said, "Boys, I'm shot through the bowels and the bladder." Luckey said, "That couldn't be, Jack, for you would be dead before this."

Root struck a match, examined the ground, and said, "It's nothing but blood."

They helped me back on my horse. We rode another mile and a half, when I had to get off again and drain my system. They helped me back, and we rode on, maybe two miles this time. "I've got to drain again," I said. I did this five times in all, and finally told them I could go no further.

They made me comfortable on my saddle blanket under a cliff of rocks. I gave each of them a watch and fifteen dollars, then made the sack into a pillow. My head was ready for it. I told them to go to Jim Dyer, who to me had proved himself a welcher, and tell him what happened to me. I told them to come back and bury me when things were favorable, as posses would soon be scouring the country for them. I said, "Put a board at my head, and write my brother in Madison County that I have crossed the Great Divide." Then, "Goodbye, boys; take care of my saddle horse as long as he lives." Luckey said, "Maybe you won't cross, Jack." I appreciated him saying that.

The boys came back the next day to bury me. It was cold and I had covered my face with a blanket, and held up two fingers to show I was still alive. Tom Root brought water from the river in his hat. Nothing ever tasted so good. They came back Thursday night [November 15] and brought me a jug of buttermilk and a pan of corn mush the Indians call *sofkey*. They also brought discouraging news—deputy marshals and Indian lighthorses were combing the Verdigris bottoms.

As they prepared to depart, I told them to bring me a syringe and a bar of Castille soap to get action on my system. They came back on Friday and worked with me all night. I was resting easy. Will Smith said he had seen five marshals searching across the river. I told them to look after themselves. They wished me well, and I them likewise. Nobody ever stood by a fallen comrade better'n they had me.

I laid there all day Saturday, Saturday night, and all day Sunday. I was beginning to feel better, and that night I pulled on my boots, used my rifle as a crutch, took the sack of money and watches and went crawling and walking the best I could through the brush. After two miles, I was weary, and rested. I took my sack (nothing was going to make me abandon that), crow-hopped down to the river, and buried it under a log.[11]

It is not known what became of the remains of the Blackstone loot. Texas Jack never mentioned it again. He finally made his way to the home of Tom Root's sister, the wife of Dick Reynolds—"another desperate character, who was then in jail at Muskogee for stealing hogs, for which crime he was afterwards convicted." Mrs. Reynolds hid Jack in a cottonfield and cared for him three days. From there, he was "conveyed in a covered wagon to Seneca, Missouri, and later to his brother in the Boston Mountains, in Arkansas."[12]

Chapter 6

. . . And the Aftermath

Nɛws of the robbery reached Fort Smith and Muskogee at 1:00 A.M. on November 14. Marshal Crump "immediately mustered a force to go to the scene, if so requested." A special train brought a squad of Muskogee deputies to Gibson Station with horses in an attached stock car. Ledbetter and Tolbert accompanied them to the scene at daybreak.[1]

The posse found the bloodstains where Texas Jack had first "drained" himself, and Bud knew that he had hit the bandit leader pretty hard. A few days later, the posse discovered Jack's resting place under the rock ledge, and tracked him to the Reynolds home. Mrs. Reynolds admitted to attending Jack's wounds, but the gang had moved on.

Marshal McAlester's deputies continued the search in the Creek Nation; Bud and Tolbert returned to duty with the railroad. At Chicago, Manager A. Antisdel of American Express lauded them for the "valiant stand made against these desperados in defense of the property in your charge . . . and I congratulate you upon and thank you for the courage and cool headedness exhibited under such trying circumstances." The express company offered a $250 reward for each robber "captured and convicted."[2]

By this time, the Muskogee authorities knew the identity of the four men they were after.

Marshal McAlester assigned Deputy Marshal Newton Le-Force, "a worthy man and a good officer," to spearhead the hunt for the bandits. LeForce learned that Root and Luckey had been seen at Root's home in the Broken Arrow settlement, fifteen miles southeast of Tulsa. Early the morning of December 5, LeForce and an Indian officer named Birchfield, with six posse-men, surrounded the place. A heavy fog blanketed the timbered bottoms. Leaving the possemen to watch the cabin, LeForce and Birchfield proceeded toward some haystacks 200 yards away, where, according to the deputy's informant, the pair would like-ly be hiding if not in the house. The dogs at the house scented the possemen and began barking. This aroused Root and Luckey and Root's wife, who were asleep in the first haystack. LeForce and Birchfield had separated and were approaching the stack between them, when Root and Luckey leaped from the hay. LeForce commanded them to surrender, returned their shots, and a running fight ensued. The possemen ran from the house, firing at the barely discernible figures as they fled. Root and Luckey escaped into the timber. When the shooting ended, LeForce lay dead, "a bullet having passed through his body from the back. His remains were taken to Muskogee for inter-ment Friday [December 7] . . . . Judge Stuart adjourned court through respect to the dead officer, and the court officials attended the funeral en masse."[3]

Marshal McAlester dispatched Deputy Will Neal to investi-gate the fight. Root's wife told Neal that her husband had received a bullet in the thigh as he fled to the woods and was being cared for by some Indian doctors, but the officer "could not locate his hiding place." Buz Luckey had gone into the "swamp lands"—the bottoms between the Arkansas and Verdi-gris rivers.[4]

Will Smith had separated from Root and Luckey shortly after the Blackstone Switch robbery. He "left the Territory . . . was never heard of again," and reportedly was "killed in a drunken brawl."[5]

The whereabouts of Texas Jack remained a mystery.

Ledbetter kept apace of developments in the pursuit of the

Blackstone bandits and continued his guard work on the Katy trains. By act of March 1, 1895, Congress wrought drastic changes in the federal court system, which recast his future as an Indian Territory lawman.

The three divisions were redesignated as "districts," and their boundaries defined. The Northern District, with headquarters at Muskogee, now comprised the Cherokee, Creek and Seminole nations and the Quawpaw Agency, the places for holding court being Muskogee, Vinita and Tahlequah, in the Cherokee Nation, and Miami, in Quawpaw country. The Central District, with headquarters at South McAlester, comprised the Choctaw Nation, the court towns being South McAlester, Atoka, Antlers, and Cameron. The Southern District, with headquarters at Ardmore, comprised the Chickasaw Nation, the court towns being Ardmore, Chikasha, Pauls Valley, and Ryan. The judges of the respective districts were again authorized to appoint commissioners, and constituted a United States Court of Appeals of Indian Territory. The oldest judge in point of commission became the chief justice of the appeals court.[6]

Section 11 of the act gave these new district courts exclusive, original jurisdiction on *all* offenses committed in Indian Territory, except cases already on docket at Fort Smith, and ended the Fort Smith court's jurisdiction over the Territory effective September 1, 1896. Though the Fort Smith court was given eighteen months grace, "it was a matter of grave doubt whether the act was a wise one . . . . Many petitions were sent to Congress for a repeal and the reinstatement of its jurisdiction, but to no avail."[7]

The act had a very depressing effect on law enforcement in Indian Territory. Of chief interest to Ledbetter, however, was the shift of Judge Stuart to the Central District, with James J. McAlester as U.S. marshal. William J. Springer, ex-Congressman from Illinois, became judge of the Northern District. Clifford Jackson was retained as district attorney. Judge Stuart resigned shortly thereafter, and was succeeded by Yancey Lewis, of Ardmore. Then Judge Springer, by virtue of holding the oldest commission, became chief justice of the court of appeals. For U.S. marshal of the Northern District at Muskogee, President Cleveland appointed Samuel Morton Rutherford.

Rutherford was a slender man with red hair and a neatly trimmed reddish mustache. He carried himself ramrod straight; his direct, searching eyes fascinated everyone he met; and he was keenly alive to his duties and responsibilities. Born in Washington County, Arkansas, in 1859, he had been educated at Cane Hill College and at Emory and Henry University in Virginia, where he was among the bachelor of arts alumni in 1883, valedictorian, and winner of the senior's debating medal. This led to his study of law in the office of Duvall & Cravens, at Fort Smith. After beginning practice in 1884, he was appointed undersheriff of Sebastian County, which position he filled until 1892, when he moved to Atoka, Choctaw Nation, to occupy for two years the position of U.S. commissioner. So he was thoroughly familiar with the conditions that vexed Indian Territory. When interviewed in Washington for the marshal appointment, he told Attorney General Richard Olney: "The Northern District will harbor no train robbers, stock thieves, timber sharks or bootleggers." His red hair almost bristled as he said it, and Olney informed President Cleveland: "I think we've found the right man."[8]

Rutherford established his home in Muskogee on March 28. Though he was six years younger than Ledbetter, Bud recognized his leadership capabilities. Rutherford was familiar with Bud's record and action at Blackstone Switch, and promptly commissioned him as one of his deputies.

Bud remained with Tolbert at Vinita, joining a corps of other long-time deputies who had become familiar figures in the town—Capt. Gideon S. White, Heck Bruner, W. C. "Bill" Smith, Dave Rusk, Enos Mills, Tom Johnson, and Charley Copeland. He scarcely had pinned on his badge when he was summoned to Fort Smith to testify in the Blackstone robbery case against Buz Luckey and Texas Jack Reed.

Reed had told his brother in Madison County that his hips had been "busted" when a horse fell on him, and his brother, knowing nothing of his outlaw record, believed him. "During the three months that I hid out, wounded and suffering, I had plenty of time to think of the past and wonder what the future held for me, and decided to make a clean breast of it all," Reed said. "I wrote Judge Parker from Madison County and he sent three deputies to get me. I was placed in the jail hospital at Fort Smith, and this was the first time I had the care of a doctor."[9]

On May 15, Reed was ushered into Judge Parker's private chambers. On a promise of clemency, he confessed the parts he and his associates played in the Blackstone holdup. He named Jim Dyer as their leader and the man who had arranged for the covered wagon to take him to Seneca, Missouri.

A week after Reed's confession, Buz Luckey was captured at the home of a relative near Choska, a Creek settlement southeast of Broken Arrow. Luckey, too, stated that Dyer had planned the robbery, but failed to show, and afterwards refused to hide him and Root on his farm, as the marshals were certain to come looking for them.

Dyer was well known to Fort Smith deputies. He had moved his family from his native Fannin County, Texas, to Indian Territory in 1884, allegedly to escape possible retribution from the many relatives of a man he had killed, though acquitted of a murder charge. For some time he had been a secret informer for the marshals—a role which, it was rumored around Wagoner, he had been forced into because, the marshals claimed, new evidence had developed in the Texas murder and the case could be brought up again. Dyer's previous record, his Wagoner friends suggested, made him an easy victim of a conspiracy.

Dyer was brought in. He denied the allegations of Reed and Luckey as "a plan conceived to swear away his liberty while securing their own." Reed countered: "What I told, I had to tell. I found God, and He gave me the strength to lisp the truth."[10]

Dyer was indicted and pleaded not guilty. Judge Parker, convinced that he had arrived at the bottom of the robbery business in that section of the Territory, set the trial for September 5 and fixed a bond at $12,000, a sum he did not believe Dyer could make. The judge, however, was "mistaken in his estimate of Dyer and misunderstood the energy and ability of Dyer's little black-haired wife." Her eyes "snapped fire" when she heard the amount and saw her husband ushered back to jail. She walked from the courtroom "with the tread of a queen," took the train to Wagoner, appeared the next day with the required bond, and took her husband home.[11]

When Ledbetter first observed Reed upon arriving at Fort Smith, the self-confident bandit was hopping about the second-floor jail corridor on crutches. Bud told Marshal Crump: "I had only a glimpse, but the moon was bright. He's the man I wounded at Blackstone Switch."

Reed ackowledged as much when interviewed in Crump's office. "Bud," he said, "that was a good shot you made with your six-shooter."

And, to Reed's amazement, Bud replied: "It wasn't a six-shooter, Jack; it was a Winchester."

The two men spent several minutes discussing their boyhood days in Madison County, and the irony of the situation—they had become "grown-ups," one a lawman, the other an outlaw.[12]

Ledbetter never had to testify against Reed. Reed and Luckey were to be tried separately from Dyer in the Blackstone robbery, but the trial was postponed in light of a new grand jury indictment charging Luckey with the murder of Deputy LeForce, and a second indictment that included Tom Root in the Blackstone holdup.

Root had recovered from his leg wound and was still hiding in the Creek Nation. Reed's confession incriminating Dyer also had opened an avenue of clemency for Root. He was induced to surrender to Deputy Jim Pettigrew the night of August 1, turned over to Marshal Rutherford at Muskogee, and transferred to Fort Smith. Root admitted his part in the train robbery, and that Dyer not only planned the affair, but "also planned the Caney, Kansas, and Bentonville, Arkansas, bank robberies conducted by Henry Starr" in March and June of 1893.[13] This added fuel to the Dyer case, which was "set aside and continued to November 5."[14]

When Root was then told that he would be charged with Buz Luckey for the murder of LeForce, he swore it was Luckey, not him, who had fired the shot that killed the deputy marshal.

Luckey was tried for the LeForce murder on August 21.

The defense "endeavored to establish that the attempt to arrest Luckey and Root was made in an unlawful manner" and they were "warranted in resisting"—despite the fact that LeForce carried a U.S. commissioner's capias for both fugitives. The defense further alleged that LeForce was "unintentionally killed by a shot from one of his assistants," as Luckey "was not on that side of the haystack when firing began." Luckey testified: "I ran out of the haystack to see what was wrong. As I was looking at what I thought was a moving object, somebody shot off my hat . . . . I answered with three or four shots, but did not fire at the man who fired at me . . . had I known the man was a marshal, I would have given up." On the contrary, Root testified for the prosecution: "When I joined Luckey in the woods, he told me he had shot the man with the overcoat on [LeForce]."[15]

There were no witnesses in Luckey's behalf. The government had nine, including Root, arrayed against him. "But Luckey's own contradictory statements were enough to convince the jury of his guilt."[16]

The big mulatto was brought before Judge Parker for sentencing on September 7. Asked if he had anything to say, he answered, "Nothing, only I never did it."

Judge Parker replied: "Twelve true and tried men of your country said that you did, and it becomes my duty to pass sentence . . . ."

He ordered Luckey to be hanged on October 20.[17]

Luckey took a writ of error to the U.S. Supreme Court. A stay of execution was issued, and while awaiting an opinion from Washington, Judge Parker handed Reed and Root a five-year sentence each on pleas of guilty with promised clemency. Reed and Root then gave joint testimony against Luckey and Jim Dyer in the Blackstone robbery case.

The Dyer-Luckey trial commenced on September 15. "So certain was Judge Parker of Dyer's guilt, and so cognizant did he become of the ability and untiring efforts of Dyer's wife in her husband's behalf, that he forbade her coming into the court room." Again Luckey had no witnesses. Dyer proved his good reputation through a number of leading Wagoner merchants, and several deputy marshals testified that he had "rendered them valuable assistance in apprehending certain noted desperados." But none could tell anything except their dealings with Dyer, nor impeach the stories of Root and Reed. Dyer and Luckey were both found guilty, and each sentenced to fifteen years in prison.[18]

Dyer appealed to the Supreme Court, his bond fixed at $8,000. The bail offered, however, was disapproved by Judge Parker after one of the principal sureties withdrew. Dyer remained in the Fort Smith jail.

On January 26, 1896, the Supreme Court reversed Luckey's murder conviction "upon confession of error by defendant in error, and cause remanded, with directions to set aside verdict and grant a new trial."[19]

Luckey's attorney lost no time in redeveloping the case. At the new trial, he produced a map three-feet square, indicating the position of the haystacks, field, fences, and cabin where the LeForce killing occurred, and the course which LeForce and his assistants ran in the direction of the stacks while firing through the fog. "By shrewd management and application of the facts on this map," he made his point and convinced the jury that, had Luckey shot LeForce, the marshal would have been "struck from the front," and that he "must have been shot unintentionally in the back by one of the possemen as they came from the house firing towards the stacks." Luckey was acquitted of murder, but he went to the penitentiary to serve fifteen years for the Blackstone robbery.[20]

Tom Root was paroled following his testimony against Luckey and Dyer. On August 31, while riding with a companion near Concharty, west of Wagoner, he was fired upon from ambush. "Root was killed instantly . . . his companion mortally wounded." The assassins were never identified or apprehended.[21]

On December 7, 1896, the Supreme Court reversed Dyer's conviction "upon confession of error by counsel for the defendant in error, the cause remanded for further proceedings in conformity to law."[22]

The reversal came less than a month after Judge Parker's death, November 17, and almost three months after the effective date of the congressional act which reduced the Fort Smith court from the greatest tribunal in history to one of comparatively petty jurisdiction over a handful of counties in western Arkansas. A number of important cases remained on the docket to be disposed of by his successor, Judge John Rogers. The Dyer case was among them.

Dyer was released under bond. In light of his past experience in relying on Wagoner merchants and his acquaintance with deputy marshals to overcome the adverse testimony of Reed and Tom Root, he and his wife spent nearly a year and a half developing new evidence for his defense.

His rehearing commenced on March 21, 1898, and lasted five days. Tom Root's widow "attempted to stick to a story . . . evidently coached into her by her husband . . . that had little weight." Dick Reynolds' wife, also a witness for the prosecution, stated: "I went to Dyer's after the robbery and got from Dyer for my brother, Tom Root, $15, a portion of the proceeds of the holdup." Defense witness testified that "the money she got was loaned to her . . . to assist Dick Reynolds," who was in jail at Muskogee for hog theft. A number of Wagoner people testified that "late on the day of the robbery Dyer ran a horse race at Wagoner . . . went home from the race track and stayed there all night." Nearly 100 letters, written by Dyer, were exhibited to show that, for a long time, he had furnished information on who was committing crimes in Indian Territory and the probable hideouts of the outlaws. One letter gave an account of the Blackstone holdup, showing that, "Instead of trying to shield the robbers, he actually was endeavoring to effect their arrest." The government offered a number of witnesses, but "Dyer's twenty-eight witnesses offset their claims." Dyer was acquitted.[23]

Reed wasn't around for the rehearing. "I was paroled out of jail on September 10,1896, to see what kind of a life I could live," he said. "Judge Parker had promised I would be released and that was done. He was a sworn enemy to people like me and he meant to clean us out, but when he gave his word it was as good as a government bond. . . . Ledbetter's shot left me limp for life. . . . I was put under supervision of federal authorities in Arizona, and every twelve months I was ready to answer my year's report. When five years rolled around I was granted a pardon— a free man."[24]

Reed became an evangelist, traveling the West preaching the consequences of outlawry and sin. He often exhibited himself with carnival companies and Wild West shows as "Texas Jack, Famous Bandit and Train Robber"—replete in a battered Stetson, high-topped boots, fringed buckskin jacket literally covered with badges and souvenirs acquired in his travels, and selling a yellow-backed pamphlet purporting to be his true life story—until his death at Tulsa in 1950.

Ledbetter frequently heard of his peregrinations. When occasionally asked about Texas Jack, he would remark: "I saw him 'hunkering' for them crossties with the sack of loot, and let him have it. That shot made a preacher out of him."[25]

Chapter 7

Two Lynchings Averted

LEDBETTER RETURNED TO Vinita from Fort Smith at the end of July 1895, when Marshal Rutherford telegraphed him to entrain at once for Catoosa, the wild, cattle-shipping town on the Frisco railroad northeast of Tulsa. An old man named Seay, a popular citizen of the place, had been murdered. Two men, W. A. Cummings and Locke Langley, were suspected of the crime, a lynching bee was in the offing, and the town authorities had requested help in quelling the trouble.

According to the story Bud received at Catoosa, Cummings had a Creek Indian wife who owned several small farms, one of which she had rented to Seay. "Seay made a crop and after laying it by went away for a while. When he returned, Cummings had taken possession and refused to let him on the place." A few days later, Seay was discovered near the Verdigris River, his throat slashed and covered with blood. Cummings claimed that after his dispute with Seay, Locke Langley and an unidentified party came to his house and "asked if he wanted to get rid of the old man." Cummings said he did, but when they "proposed to put a rock around Seay's neck and throw him into the river," he disagreed—"said it would be murder"—and never saw Seay afterwards until his body was found in the woods "all bloody." Cummings was "a bad man . . . accustomed to harboring outlaws"; the people thought he "told his story to defend himself . . . that he and Langley had murdered Seay," and they were in the mood to mob them.[1]

Bud took Cummings and Langley into custody. He promised they would be taken to Muskogee and transferred to Fort Smith to be dealt with in Judge Parker's court. The people threatened to take the prisoners from him.

Bud telegraphed a deputy at Tulsa to come assist in removing the prisoners safely. But it proved unnecessary. Word spread that Bud was the officer who had killed Joe McNally and "shot up" Texas Jack, and was so adept with a Winchester that he "could shoot the lobe off a man's ear and never put a mark on his jaw." Before the Tulsa deputy arrived, "the people decided to let the law take its course." Bud departed on the Frisco with Cummings and Langley in tow, without incident.[2]

Bud delivered his prisoners to Marshal Rutherford the evening of August 6, and found the marshal's office and Muskogee in "a swirl of excitement." A new outlaw gang, led by a full blood of the Euchee band of Creek Indians, named Rufus Buck, had sprung up in the Duck and Snake creek areas southeast of Tulsa. The people in the country west of Muskogee were "in constant fear of being robbed or abused by them. . . . Many of the homes were under guard of the men folk, and the town of Okmulgee had its guns greased and loaded [should] the gang visit that place."[3]

Besides Buck, the gang consisted of Luckey Davis, Sam Sampson, and Maomi July, Creek full-bloods and half-bloods of the Cussetah tribal town (Tulsa); and Lewis Davis, a black Creek. Supposedly bent on running intruding white farmers, cattleman, and timber dealers out of the Creek Nation, the crimes they had already committed during their few days of existence were unequalled in the annals of Indian Territory brigandage.

In the early morning hours of July 29, the gang had stolen several good horses west of Checotah and some saddles from the town's livery stable, which they left in flames. Attempting to rob a store at Okmulgee the evening of July 30, they gunned down City Marshal John Garrett. The night of August 3, they burned the houses of the Pigeon Family of Indians, who allegedly were white sympathizers. On August 4, near Natura, southeast of

Tulsa, they attacked a white man named Ayers and his young daughter, who were moving cross-country in a wagon, threatened to kill Ayers, and mass-raped the girl. On Berryhill Creek, within eight miles of Okmulgee, they abused a timber dealer named Shafey for nearly an hour, finally voted not to kill him, and took his cash, jewelry, horse, and saddle. At dusk they swept down on Benton Callahan and a black cowboy driving some cattle southeast of Okmulgee; badly wounded the cowboy and killed his horse; shot off part of Callahan's left ear; robbed him of his hat, boots, horse, and saddle; and stampeded the cattle. Fleeing back northwest, they rode to the Gus Chambers ranch on Duck Creek at midnight to obtain fresh horses. Chambers resisted with a shotgun and rifle, and they filled his house with lead. On August 5, near Wealaka, they ravished an elderly widow and rifled her household goods which she was moving in two wagons from one farm to another; then raided the camp of a white man and killed him near the Half Moon Ranch between Okmulgee and Checotah. That night, they proceeded to a home west of Checotah where a white schoolmistress was boarding and outraged the teacher.*

Copies of federal warrants issued at Fort Smith on August 6, charging the Buck gang with the murder of Garrett and assault to kill Benton Callahan and his cowboy, had been dispatched to Marshal Rutherford. Shortly before Ledbetter arrived in Muskogee with his Catoosa prisoners, the marshal "sent twelve of a total of eighteen deputies in the Northern District into the field to put 'Buck and Co.' out of business." News had been received that the "Ayers girl raped by the gang has died," and that early that morning, the Bucks had committed their most heinous crime at the home of the Henry Hassan family on Snake Creek.[4]

Henry Hassan had disagreed with Rufus Buck's ideas for disposing of whites, and Buck came to square his grudge. After looting the house and forcing Hassan's wife, Rosetta, to prepare them a meal, the gang forced the woman into the barn, where

---

*The Buck gang's depredations are fully described in Glenn Shirley, *13 Days of Terror: The Rufus Buck Gang in Indian Territory* (Barbed Wire Press, Stillwater, Oklahoma, 1996).

each took his turn raping her while the others held Hassan at bay with six-shooters and rifles. They then marched Hassan and his hired man to a spring on Snake Creek, threw them in the water, made them fight each other until nearly exhausted, and galloped away, warning Hassan never to appear as a witness against them.

A posse was within three miles of the Hassan farm, but did not learn of the attack until an hour or so later. Mrs. Hassan had dragged herself from the barn into a cornfield, where her husband found her, babbling half out of her mind, and rushed her to a doctor. Deputy Marshals Samuel Haynes and N. B. Irwin were spearheading hundreds of citizens—Indians, whites, and blacks alike—who had "turned out to hunt the outlaws down," and Capt. Edmund Harry had entered the field with his light-horse police, in full force. "Every hill, every bottom and every trail for miles around was being critically searched, and there was hardly a hope for the escape of the brutes."[5]

Though jurisdiction in the Seay murder case at Catoosa rested with the Muskogee court, Judge Parker still held jurisdiction in such cases, and Marshal Rutherford chose to deliver all major law violators to Fort Smith. Accordingly, he ordered Ledbetter to deliver his prisoners to Marshal Crump, file his papers, and return to Muskogee as soon as possible for assignment in the field against the Bucks.

Bud completed his mileage and complaint work with the Fort Smith district attorney and U.S. Commissioners Court Thursday morning, August 8. Marshal Crump had received a new dispatch on the Bucks. Wednesday afternoon the gang had held up the big Norburg & Company store in the sawmill village of Arkekochee at the extreme northeastern corner of the Seminole Nation, below the North Fork of the Canadian. Recrossing the river, they had robbed a store in the hamlet of McDermott, the Knobble general store, just west of well-guarded Okmulgee, and fled northward into the hills.

At about 1:00 in the afternoon, while Bud was waiting to board the train for Muskogee, another dispatch arrived at Fort Smith. The Bucks had been surprised in camp seven miles north of Okmulgee by Deputies Haynes and Irwin, Captain Harry, and his lighthorse police. The gang had fled to a nearby knob called "Flat Rock," had been surrounded by the officers and nearly 100 other manhunters, and were engaged in a fierce battle with no chance of escape.

The contents of the dispatch "found its way to every nook and cranny of the city." As it reached the courthouse, where an unusually large number of cases were being disposed of by Judge Parker and over 400 witnesses and spectators filled the yard and corridors, there was "secret exultation at the fact that the murderous and unholy gang had been tracked to their lair. . . . And when court finally adjourned everyone hurried to the streets to learn of any later news of the fight, and gathered in little knots to discuss the probable outcome."[6]

Shortly after dark, a third dispatch was received stating that the battle was over. Rufus Buck, Luckey Davis, Sam Sampson, and Maomi July had been captured; Lewis Davis, wounded in one leg, had managed to escape.

Ledbetter reached Muskogee on Friday evening, August 9. The marshal's office swirled with excitement as never before. Paden Tolbert was there. "Glad you're back, Bud," he said. "We need your services."

The people tried to lynch the four Bucks after they were brought into Okmulgee. Haynes, Irwin, and Captain Harry were smuggling them down Okmulgee Creek to the Canadian that night and bringing them to Muskogee, where more trouble was expected.

The Bucks were loaded on the Katy train at Oktaha, as arranged by Marshal Rutherford. At midnight they were in the Muskogee jail on North Third Street.

The jail was a story-and-a-half wooden affair with a heavy entrance door, surrounded by a strong stockade of pickets with a wooden gate little higher than a man's head. Saturday, August 10, was visitor's day at the jail. The stockade gate was opened, and Ledbetter and Tolbert stood guard while scores of people were admitted in small groups to view the prisoners in their cell. Many left, angrily muttering disappointment that the four had not been lynched at Okmulgee.

The people conducted themselves in an orderly fashion during the day. About 6:00 P.M., Benton Callahan, Henry Hassan, and old man Ayers, whose daughter had been outraged

and died, arrived in the city. These "aggrieved parties" were
merely en route to Fort Smith to testify before the grand jury,
but "their presence lent vigor to the mob advocates." By nightfall, "it was pretty well understood that a mob would be organized. Rumor came that a strong band would come in from the
country for the purpose. . . . People from all over the town
began to bunch together under the arc light on Main Street,
until the street was almost blockaded. . . . Meanwhile, Marshal
Rutherford had put a strong guard in the stockade, and
expressed determination that the prisoners should be protected. . . . Directly, the crowd began to move on to the jail . . ."[7]

Ledbetter and Tolbert were positioned on each side of the
gate, six-shooters and Winchesters ready for any action necessary. Marshal Rutherford and Chief Deputy McDonald stood on
an empty supply wagon that had been pulled up just inside, and
as the crowd approached, they appeared above the pickets, shot-
guns cradled in their arms.

The mob halted. McDonald "made an earnest talk which
made the crowd waiver"—the Bucks would be protected with
the same zeal and determination with which they had been
apprehended. Rutherford "followed in an appeal for the crowd
to disperse . . . he appreciated the indignation and feeling which
impelled the people to arise against the prisoners, but the
majesty of the law must be preserved at any cost." He assured
them the prisoners would be taken to Fort Smith where justice
could be dealt out legally. When he referred to Judge Parker as
"a certain punisher of crime," several cheered. But the crowd
remained adamant. Rutherford still held a trump card—and he
played it. "Don't you see who's guarding this gate?" he shouted,
pointing to Ledbetter and Tolbert. "You know these men—you
might carry out your plan and lynch the prisoners, but some of
you will die! The life of one of you or one of the guards is worth
more than the whole coop of prisoners." Slowly the crowd
"broke away, and directly all were moving back towards town."
By midnight, "most everybody was abed, but some of the boys
were out for a hanging and determined to have one. So they
stuffed a dummy and hung it on an electric light pole in front of
the Patterson Mercantile Co. Sunday morning . . . without fur-

ther trouble . . . the prisoners were carried to Fort Smith, and the dummy was laid to rest."[8]

Fort Smith was going to church when Rutherford and his deputies marched Rufus Buck, Luckey Davis, Sam Sampson, and Maomi July from the railroad station down Garrison Avenue in chains to the federal prison. It was a spectacle the city never forgot. Next day, Lewis Davis was captured by Deputy Irwin and Tom Grayson of the Creek lighthorse at the home of an Indian family, eight miles west of the Flat Rock fight. In September all five Bucks were tried for the rape of Rosetta Hassan. They were convicted and hanged in unison on July 1, 1896.

The outcome of the Seay murder case is not known. It apparently was among many other U.S. district and commissioners court records that have been lost down the years, and stories of Ledbetter's exploits make no further mention of the case.

Nonetheless, Bud had averted a lynching at Catoosa and helped save the necks of the Buck gang for the gibbet.

Chapter 8

Bringing in the Turners
and the Greens

THE PEOPLE IN THE Northern District always looked forward to the annual "stomp dance" that was held during the latter part of August in the Hominy and Bird creek bottoms, ten miles north of Tulsa. Indians came from as far away as Shawnee and Tecumseh, in Oklahoma Territory, and Wewoka, Creek Nation — the young bucks on horseback and old men and women and children in two-seated hacks and light wagons, "bringing their tepees, bedding, all the dogs, dance costumes, and medicine bag." Beeves were slaughtered and distributed to each tepee. "What the Indians didn't eat and the flies didn't carry off, the dogs got." Three to five hundred Indians in native dress took part in the all-night programs, "beating tom-tom and rattling the turtle shell." Many whites also attended and were provided a platform on which to perform old-time square dances.[1]

Deputies Ledbetter, B. "Bea" Mellon, and William Frank Jones (a twenty-three-year-old deputy working under his uncle, Jesse H. Jones of Checotah) were assigned to "work the dance" and assist Indian police in "watching for bootleggers." Despite the presence of the officers, there were "several fist fights and much drinking."[2]

Alec Daniels and Henry Childers had two jugs of whiskey on the grounds, and met Frank Sennett. Daniels and Sennett,

49

enemies for years, "renewed their quarrel in a drunken brawl. Sennett beat Daniels to the draw, killed him, and Lon Cannady, a friend of Daniels, then shot Sennett," who died as Ledbetter and the other deputies reached the scene.

Childers was looking for Cannady and "trying to run off with the whiskey." Mellon attempted to arrest him, but Childers "leaped on his horse, making a wild dash through the crowd." Indians and whites scattered in every direction. "Fearing that many people would be injured," Mellon yelled for Childers to halt, but Childers "kept spurring his horse," and Mellon cut down on him with his Winchester. Childers fell from his saddle, dead.

Sam Childers, Henry's brother, arrived on the grounds. Sam had "plenty nerve" and began rounding up some of the boys for more bloodshed. Ledbetter, "knowing the consequences of such a battle," called Sam to one side and, in his cool, forceful manner, told the would-be avenger: "Start anything like that and you are the first man I will kill. The best thing for you to do is take Henry's body home and let the Indian Police settle the whole matter." Sam Childers took Bud's advice.[3]

For more than a year the Turner gang had ranged the hills between Sapulpa and Mann's Ford (Mannford) on the Cimarron, in the northwestern corner of the Creek Nation. They stole cattle and horses and robbed small stores in the Osage reservation above the Arkansas and westward in Oklahoma Territory. In June 1894 a squad of Muskogee marshals had corralled the gang below the Cimarron. "The band, when it saw how it was outnumbered, ran away. The officers brought in 229 head of cattle, 80 head of horses, and three Negro suspects who were attending the holding place."[4]

The gang consisted of brothers Al and Lon Turner and two former Turkey Track ranch cowboys, Bob Cloud and Jim Pendleton. Marshal Rutherford was informed of their new hangout —the Jane Wolf ranch on Salt Creek, "surrounded by high bluffs," about ten miles southwest of Sapulpa. He handed Ledbetter a commissioners warrant for their arrest, and Bud enlisted young Frank Jones "to help bring them in."

Bud and Frank were outfitting in Muskogee for their expedition, when Frank was sought out by a man named Sam Bell, a cattle rustler Frank had known in Texas a couple of years before while foreman on the Bill Jackson ranch between Belton and San Angelo. Bell, as always, was on the scout— this time on a federal charge in the Eastern District of Texas. "I've been in touch with the Turner gang and am considered one of their number," he told Frank. "I can turn that gang to you, if you can help me out of my trouble." Bud and Frank decided "it would be a good thing to line him up . . . have him report the gang's course of action," and promised to do what they could to get him "off the hook." Marshal Rutherford agreed to pay Bell's expenses from federal funds as a "stool pigeon."

Bud and Frank entrained with their pack horses to Sapulpa, and established a secret camp on Salt Creek, within walking distance of the Jane Wolf ranch. Bell joined the Turners, and rode off with the gang on a foray into Oklahoma Territory.

Bud and Frank waited a week for Bell to report. Each night they "slipped close to the ranch house, lay down, fought mosquitoes big as horseflies, and went back to camp." On the seventh day, their patience worn thin, they decided to do some fishing, and soon had a string of black bass. That evening, when Frank had fried the fish to a crisp golden brown and Bud's Dutch-oven bread was almost done, "the bushes parted and out stepped Bell." The outlaws had just ridden in; Pendleton was nursing a slight gunshot wound received in their last escapade; all four were in the house, "well-armed and drinking."

It was all Bud and Frank wanted to know. They grabbed their Winchesters and headed for the house, running.

The structure was a double log cabin connected by a breezeway, called a "dog trot," which allowed cooler air to pass through on hot summer days. Bud leaped into the door of one cabin, Frank into the other. When they met in the breezeway a few moments later, each had two prisoners, handcuffed.

They were ready to begin their trip to Muskogee with the Turner brothers, Pendleton and Cloud, but had to pick up their camping outfit. And this was the tragic part of their expedition. They found their fish truly were *black* bass. In their haste to capture the outlaws, they had forgotten to take the fish off the fire.

Bud and Frank spent the night at Sapulpa, and took their prisoners to Muskogee the next day. The Turners, Pendleton, and Cloud were tried for robbery and stock thievery and each were given fifteen years in the penitentiary. Pendleton served two years of his sentence and died in prison of tuberculosis.

Reminiscing about the capture of the Turners afterwards, Bud and Frank wondered if it was really worth giving up that skillet full of fish.

As for Sam Bell, Marshal Rutherford gave him a government check for $100. Bell returned to Texas with the understanding that he would be given a suspended sentence if he gave himself up, but somehow the arrangement went awry. "He was met by officers as soon as he entered Texas territory, and killed. The check was found on him—he had not even had time to cash it."[5]

Bud wasn't pleased over the fate of Sam Bell. But it was not the last time he would enlist an informer to bring outlaws to justice. In October 1896 he used this means to round up the Green gang.

This gang consisted of three brothers: Bill Green, age 21; Ed, a year or so younger; and Arthur, still in his teens. The family had come into the Cooweescoowee District of the Cherokee Nation in the early 1880s and obtained a small farm deep in the bottoms between the Caney and Verdigris rivers, about six miles west of Oologah, a coal-mining, cattle-shipping center on the Arkansas Valley railroad. The mother died in the mid-1880s, and tall, long-whiskered "Old Man" Green married a full-blooded Indian woman, who "took her stepchildren to heart like a mother cat with kittens." Bill and Ed were old enough to take riding jobs on Ed Halsell's Mashed-O ranch, which "spread pretty much all over that country," and were top cowhands when the Halsell outfit pulled up stakes for Colorado in the early 1890s. Afterwards, Bill and Ed "just drifted," and Arthur followed them. Cattle disappeared from the far-flung rangelands— "a steer here, two there, a few calves." The location of the Green farm was ideal for a "wide-loop" spread and, as neighboring ranchers and cowboys observed, "it grew too fast for the natural offspring of a few cows the family owned." Nothing was pinned on the brothers, however, and the Indian stepmother would "severely tongue-lash" anyone who accused "her boys" of any wrong-doing.[6]

In September 1896 the brothers "became out-and-out out-laws." They rode to the L. J. Snarr coal works northwest of Oologah, "lined the working men up in a row, " including Snarr himself, and "frisked their pockets." The robbery netted only $28, so they held up a store at Ringold, west of the Caney River. This holdup proved to be a "water-haul," and Arthur was wounded in the hip. Bill and Ed hid him in the home of a friend, Milt Barker, then attempted to hold up the store of D. H. Leerskov on Posey Creek, below the Arkansas. Again, they were repulsed. Leerskov suffered three wounds, none serious, and the Greens fled, leaving $4 of their own money on one of the counters in the store.[7]

Posses hunted the robbers for several days without finding a trace of them. Arthur remained at the Barker home, nursing his injured hip, and Bill and Ed murdered a man named George Walden, who lived thirty miles north of Tulsa.

The Walden killing was primarily the result of a quarrel with Milt Barker over an Indian woman, Minnie Locket. Walden and Barker had traded wives. After the trade, Walden learned that Minnie was due $500 from the sale of some Shawnee lands in Kansas, and demanded the wives "be swapped back." Barker refused, figuring he was entitled to the money since Minnie now lived with him, and offered to split the $500 with Bill and Ed Green to murder Walden. Bill rode over to Walden's camp one evening, saying, "I'm hungry." Walden's wife fixed him a plate of bacon and eggs. After supper, he invited Walden outside where his horse was tied. "I want to talk to you," he said. "I have a jug of whiskey." When Walden stepped outside, Ed Green slipped from his hiding place behind the tent and shot him.[8]

When the word reached Muskogee, Marshal Rutherford sent Ledbetter to apprehend Walden's killers. Bud picked up Deputy Lon Lewis, at Tulsa. Lon deputized his twenty-one-year-old brother, S. R. Lewis, as his posseman.

S. R. recalled: "We went to Buck Creek. . . . Walden's wife told us how the killing took place. . . . We searched for the Green boys on the Caney and in the eastern part of the Osage Nation . . . found no clue about where they were hiding. Finally we disbanded. . . . A week later we again took the trail . . . went on the Caney River not far from the Green boys' home to the home of a man named Osborne. Lon sent for Charles M. McClelland [a well-known Indian scout, who ranched east of Oologah]. Mc-Clelland came to Osborne's home and a plan was framed to capture the Green boys. The man chosen was Charles Leonard Trainor. . . ."⁹

Trainor, a cowboy on the McClelland ranch, was under indictment for stealing cattle. The Greens knew of his trouble, and Ledbetter assured him the charges would be dropped if he could "gain their confidence and put them in the hands of the marshals." McClelland, anxious to put an end to rustling in the area, approved the plan, and "a deal was made." Trainor went to Old Man Green, told him the law was "nippin' at his heels," and asked to "scout" with his sons. The old man "took him south of where Collinsville now stands to the boys' hideout." Arthur had recovered from his wound and was riding with Bill and Ed again. Trainor informed them of an arrangement he allegedly had made to rob the big store of Ed Sunday & Son, at Oologah, Monday evening, October 12. Trainor's mother lived on the Verdigris east of Ash Hopper ford, southeast of Oologah, so Trainor suggested they go there for a good meal, and afterwards, he would take them to a pasture on the McClelland ranch where they could get fresh horses and ride to Oologah before the store's closing time. "The boys fell for the plan and agreed to go with him." Trainor then told them he also had made arrangements to rob the bank at Chelsea, northeast of Oologah on the Frisco railroad, and needed to go to Chelsea alone to check the bank's layout "for accuracy." Instead, Trainor "rendezvoused at Osborne's farm with the marshals . . . two o'clock in the afternoon was fixed as the time the gang would cross the river at Ash Hopper ford."¹⁰

Ledbetter and Lon Lewis assembled a posse at Osborne's farm the bleak morning of October 12. S. R. Lewis was there. McClelland came, bringing a Cherokee associate, Smith Bushyhead. Deputy Marshal Bob O'Bryan of Wagoner completed the party.

The posse reached Ash Hopper ford about 1:00 P.M., concealed their horses in the timber, and divided into two groups. It was understood that Trainor would lead the Greens to the east side of the river. S. R. Lewis, Osborne, and O'Bryan remained in the timber as back-ups. Bud, Lon Lewis, McClelland, and Bushyhead hid at the top of the river back behind several big logs that had been washed up at floodstage, where the demand was to be made to surrender.

At 2:00 P.M. horses were heard on the trail. As the Greens rode down to the ford in single file, Trainor dropped behind them. "The boys must have suspected something, for they made Trainor ride ahead . . . made him ride Bill Green's gray horse and even put Bill's overcoat and hat on him. Trainor must have thought he was a goner, but he had to take a chance. . . ." He rode into the stream, allowed his horse to drink, then "rode out on the east side where there were some flat rocks." Ledbetter and his party behind the logs above "would have killed him had it not been for McClelland's sharp eyes." McClelland recognized Trainor, despite his garb, and "passed the word down the line of officers." The Greens followed Trainor across the stream. Arthur dismounted on the flat rocks and laid down on his stomach to drink. Trainor said, "Ed, you and Bill ride up and see what you can see." Bill and Ed started up the bank and were confronted by Ledbetter's party. "Throw up your hands, boys!" Bud shouted. The Greens went for their rifles.[11]

S. R. Lewis summarized how the battle ended:

"Lon's rifle spoke first, shooting Bill. . . . McClelland's double-barreled shotgun got Ed, but didn't kill him. It was only loaded with turkey shot. Ed fell to the ground, rolled onto the rocks and began firing with his pistols. . . . Ledbetter fired the shot that stopped Ed. Smith Bushyhead shot Arthur through the upper part of his lungs. Bill and Ed both died."[12]

The dead and wounded were hauled into Oologah in a hack obtained from George Hoak, a nearby farmer. Bill and Ed Green were laid out in the Otis Skidmore building and buried in the old Musgrove cemetery west of town the next day — in the same coffin and the same grave. Their father and Indian stepmother wanted it that way.

Oologah physicians announced that Arthur would live. He was taken to Muskogee, where he was able to prove he was at Milt Barker's home nursing his injured hip when Walden was killed, and thus avoided a charge of murder. He was given five years in the Fort Leavenworth, Kansas, penitentiary for the

Ringold robbery, served his term, and died a few years later due to his lung wound, in New Mexico. Barker was convicted for procuring assassins in Walden's death. Charles Leonard Trainor eventually went to Hollywood, where he often appeared in Western movies. "He was a friend of Will Rogers, and his particular pleasure was to care for Will's favorite horse."[13]

Ledbetter went after one other gang in closing his activities for 1896.

Some hog and cow thieves, Arch Landrum, Tobe Lynch, John Towers, and John Starr, were operating along the Grand River in the hills adjacent to Bolen's ferry. "A terrible state of affairs," the Vinita *Indian Chieftain* termed it. The black thieves "schemed to steal a pen of fat hogs from Jim Yost, drive them into the woods and butcher them in the night." Their final act was "stealing and butchering a steer belonging to Tom Brown, at the ferry."

The hide from Brown's animal was discovered and identified. Friday night, November 27, Ledbetter and his posse found the trail of the thieves, which led to the house of one of the four parties. Looking through the window, Bud saw one of the men frying beef. "He made known the fact that he was an officer, and demanded that the door be opened. . . . This request was refused, and Mr. Ledbetter pried the door open with his Winchester, and stepped inside in time to cover the man before he could get a gun, which he was trying to do. A quantity of beef was being cooked on the fire and quite a quantity was found in the loft—albeit the Negroes declared they were cooking the very last in the house." The culprits were taken to Vinita. "The preliminary examination was held before Commissioner McClure Tuesday evening [December 1] and concluded Wednesday morning; all were held, bond fixed at $1,000 which they failed to give and were remanded to jail."[14]

The thieves were later convicted and given jail terms at Muskogee for the theft of Tom Brown's cow.

The year 1896 also ended the Parker era at Fort Smith, leaving the Northern, Central, and Southern district courts with full jurisdiction over federal offenses committed in Indian Territory.

Chapter 9

A New U.S. Marshal and a Rapist Named Brooks

The ELECTION OF WILLIAM McKinley in 1896 as the twenty-fifth president of the United States was the harbinger of another "political resetting of the docket" in Indian Territory.[1] His appointments following inauguration on March 4, 1897, changed many official faces, and considering the action of the 55th Congress, which convened on March 15, "one might well have believed the federal government was becoming Indian Territory mad."[2]

By act of June 7, Congress virtually made useless the tribal courts. It gave the U.S. courts "original and exclusive jurisdiction and the authority to try and determine all civil cases in law and equity and all criminal cases for the punishment of offenses committed . . . by *any* person" in the Territory; gave U.S. commissioners "the power and jurisdiction . . . as respects all persons and property," applying the laws of the United States and Arkansas "in force therein . . . *irrespective of race*"; declared "any citizen of any one of the Five Civilized Tribes, otherwise qualified, to be competent to serve as juror in any of the said courts"; and provided that "all acts, ordinances and resolutions of the councils of the Five Civilized Tribes shall be immediately certified, on their passage, to the President of the United States." Further, the act provided for the appointment of an additional, or supernumerary judge, for the Territory, to hold court "at the town of Wagoner, and at such other places as the appellate court [Court of Appeals of Indian Territory] shall determine."[3]

Another Congressional act, approved June 30, enlarged the scope of the laws against introducing whiskey into Indian Territory by including "beer, ale and wine, or any ardent or other intoxicating liquor whatever, or any essence, extract, bitters, preparation, compound, composition or any article whatever under any name, label or brand, which produces intoxication."[4]

Thereafter, Bud Ledbetter and his fellow deputies would devote much of their time to enforcing this prohibition.

For the supernumerary judgeship, President McKinley appointed John Robert Thomas, ex-Congressman from Illinois, who had strongly supported his bid for the White House. Springer remained judge of the Northern District, Rutherford as U.S. Marshal, and Pliny L. Soper of Kansas succeeded Clifford Jackson as U.S. attorney. The big shake-up of judges, prosecuting attorneys, and U.S. marshals occurred in the Central and Southern districts. Jasper P. Grady became U.S. marshal at South McAlester, and John S. Hamer, the U.S. marshal at Ardmore.[5]

These changes were of little consequence to Ledbetter, except that Judge Thomas was empowered, as were the other judges, to hold court in any of the districts as necessity required, and as he traveled the Northern District from one court town to another, Bud often served as one of the attachés, providing protection to the court and executing any precept directed to him. Judge Thomas respected the abilities of his fellow jurists and sat twice a year with two of the district judges on the court of appeals to review decisions of the trial courts. He became Bud's favorite judge.

Bud's personal concern, however, was the removal of Marshal Rutherford and the appointment on September 21, 1897, of Dr. Leo E. Bennett as U.S. Marshal at Muskogee.

Bennett was born in Kansas in November 1857, the son of Dr. James E. and Martha A. Bennett. Dr. James Bennett had relocated his family to Fort Smith, where Leo had attended public schools. Later Leo attended the prestigious Rugby Academy in Wilmington, Delaware, the University of Michigan at Ann Arbor, and finally graduated from medical school of the University of Tennessee at Nashville, to follow in the footsteps of his father. He began his practice in 1883 in the Creek Nation, at Eufaula, where he also engaged in stock-raising, politics, and the newspaper business. In 1887 he was appointed federal agent for the Five Civilized Tribes at Muskogee, at the same time operating a store north of Muskogee on the Katy railroad. He made frequent trips to Washington and successfully obtained a post office at the growing little switchyard, Gibson Station. Seeing that Muskogee was destined to become the metropolis of the Territory, he resigned as Indian agent, sold his interest in the Eufaula *Indian Journal,* moved to Muskogee and launched the *Phoenix* on property he obtained by trading advertising space in his newspaper. The *Phoenix* became one of the Territory's leading newspapers, and in 1893, Bennett was named president of the newly formed Indian Territory Press Association.[6]

Why the doctor accepted active involvement in law enforcement over his medical career puzzled Ledbetter. Apparently, it was Bennett's abilities as a planner and administrator that attracted President McKinley. To Bud, it was his prestige and influence in the Territory. In turn, the new marshal, who often had carried Ledbetter's exploits in his newspapers, looked on Bud with a jaundiced eye—perhaps a twinge of jealousy. Nevertheless, he retained Bud along with most of Rutherford's seasoned and capable officers, and increased to twenty-four the number of deputies serving the Northern District.

Marshal Bennett had hardly finished selecting his force on October 29, when he was notified that a black man named K. B. Brooks had raped and almost beaten to death a young girl at Hudson, on the Big Creek tributary of the Verdigris. Brooks was at large somewhere on Big Creek or in the Verdigris bottoms.

Bennett challenged Bud: "If you're so good, why don't you bring in K. B. Brooks?"

Bud replied quietly: "I'll attend to it—right away."

Bud entrained home to Vinita, assembled his camping outfit, and proceeded to Hudson on horseback. He learned that Brooks had come from Paris, Texas, to the Cherokee Nation and found work as a hired hand for a white man named Combs. Combs was the father of three motherless daughters—Lulu, sixteen, Cora, eleven, and Ida, a baby of five. On October 28 he had gone to Kansas on a business trip, leaving the children in Brooks' care.

At bedtime the children retired together in one room. About midnight, Brooks went to the house, armed with a club, and entered the room where the children were sleeping. This awakened Lulu; she called to her sister Cora to light a lamp. Brooks fell upon the bed and seized her. She fought him and screamed until he clubbed her into unconsciousness. Cora grabbed the baby and fled from the house into some trees. Brooks searched for them, failed to find them, and returned to the bedroom. Lulu had recovered sufficiently to steal away, but he found her, in a half-dazed condition, a few yards from the house. Again Brooks wielded his club until it broke into three pieces. While the girl lay helpless and almost dead, he ravished her, then fled.

Meanwhile, Cora carried her baby sister to the home of a neighbor, who alerted the entire community. Lulu was rushed to a doctor, while every man and boy around Hudson searched for Brooks.

Bud picked up Brooks' trail at the home of Moore Gibson, about three miles from Hudson. Gibson related how Brooks had come in the night, borrowed a blanket, and asked to sleep in his barn until morning. At breakfast, Moore questioned him about the blood on his hands, and he replied: "I slapped Lulu Combs' face, an I'm leavin' the country." He had taken the road west to Lenapah.

Bud traced Brooks across the Verdigris to Lenapah, thence across the Caney River near Bartlesville. Following the fugitive like a bloodhound, he finally overtook him on Sandy Creek, in the Osage reservation, and delivered him to Muskogee on November 9.[7]

Lon R. Stansbery, Ledbetter's biographer, commented: "Bud was out in the wilds so long after this man that when he did get back to civilization he needed an ensilage cutter instead of a razor."[8]

Brooks was promptly arraigned on a charge of rape before U.S. Commissioner W. C. Jackson, and committed to the Muskogee jail pending examination for indictment by a grand jury.

Then Bud was riding again—this time against a bandit quintet known as the Jennings gang.

Chapter 10

Rampage of the Jennings Gang

The Jennings quintet consisted of twenty-three-year-old, pint-sized, red-haired Al Jennings; his thirty-year-old, hulking brother, Frank; brothers Pat and Morris O'Malley; and Richard "Little Dick" West, a remnant of the old Bill Doolin gang. Except for West, all were rank amateurs.

Al and Frank were the younger sons of J. D. F. Jennings, of Tazewell County, Virginia, a former Methodist circuit rider and surgeon during the Civil War. After the war, J. D. F. Jennings relocated his family to Illinois, studied law, and for the next several years practiced in Illinois, Ohio (where his wife died), Missouri, Kansas, and Colorado, serving occasionally as a prosecuting attorney and county judge. In 1889 he participated in the Oklahoma "land rush," securing a claim southeast of Kingfisher. Two older sons, Ed and John, accompanied him. Frank, at the time, was deputy clerk in the district court at Denver. Ed and John had learned enough law in their father's office to set up practice at El Reno, Canadian County. Al, a graduate of the law department of the West Virginia State University, soon joined Ed and John. In 1892 Al was elected prosecuting attorney of Canadian County. All the Jenningses were active in Democratic politics, and with the opening of the Cherokee Outlet in 1893, the father was appointed as the first probate judge of newly organized Woodward County, at Woodward. Ed and John moved their practice to Woodward, and Al rejoined them following his defeat for reelection in November 1894.

Al's excuse for taking the bandit trail was the killing of his brother Ed by Temple Houston, the flamboyant, long-haired gun-lawyer son of Gen. Sam Houston, first president of the Republic of Texas. Ed and John Jennings incurred Houston's displeasure during a lawsuit between two cattlemen over pasture rent in the summer of 1895. Again, on October 8, Ed clashed with Houston over a number of points while defending a case involving a theft from the Santa Fe railroad, represented by Houston. Houston accused him of being grossly ignorant of the law, and Ed, slamming his fist on the table, shouted: "You're a damned liar!" Guns were drawn; only the prompt interference of bystanders prevented their use. The court rebuked both attorneys; they apologized, but their tempers seethed. That evening, in the Cabinet Saloon, Ed and John Jennings renewed the quarrel with Houston. Few words were spoken before gunfire erupted. John, his gun arm shot away, ran outside and reached his home after fainting once from loss of blood. Ed, shot in the head, died almost instantly. Houston was tried and acquitted for killing Ed, the evidence indicating that his bullet which tore into John's arm had caused John to shoot his brother in the head.

Al claimed cold-blooded murder; that society favored famous people. Frank came down from Denver. He and Al pooled their resources, saddled their horses, and left Woodward, as Al related afterwards, "to establish some base" from which to kill Houston. "We became outlaws in spirit . . . the rest came as gradually and easy as sliding down hill."

Broken by the traumatic loss of Ed, Judge Jennings moved to Shawnee, where he continued to practice law. In the populist victory of 1896, he was elected probate judge of Pottawatomie County, and moved to Tecumseh. John, permanently crippled from the Woodward tragedy, became probate clerk for his father. Judge Jennings was reelected to a second term in 1898, but the lasting stigma placed on his reputation by the activities of Al and Frank ultimately ended his political career. In 1901 he moved to Slater, Missouri, where he died in June 1903, at age seventy.

For months, Al and Frank rode about the country "hunting" Temple Houston but never meeting him—perhaps, because they remembered his quickness and accuracy with a six-shooter, and because Houston made not the least effort to avoid them. In any event, they never returned to Woodward, and often were seen around Shawnee and Tecumseh consorting with the O'Malleys.

The O'Malleys have been written off as a couple of "plow-pushers." On the contrary, Morris had served as a deputy and Pat as posseman under U.S. Marshal E. D. Nix of Oklahoma Territory, until the Department of Justice ordered them discharged in 1895 for padding witness and mileage accounts. Al admired the brothers as "two wild Irish boys, who knew nothing but fight and didn't care a damn for anything else."

Through the O'Malleys, Al and Frank found employment on the Spike S ranch of John Harless (some four miles south of present Bixby), in the Creek Nation. Harless had the reputation of rustling other people's livestock. A large, red barn was the ranch's landmark. A wooded mountain range to the south and the heavily thicketed bottom of Snake Creek to the east afforded easy escape routes for the hard characters that frequented the Spike S domain. Here Little Dick West entered the picture, and the Jennings gang, per se, was nurtured.

Since Bill Doolin's death in 1896, West had avoided capture by holing up with a Creek Indian woman on the North Canadian across from Old Watsonville (present Dustin). He also spent a great deal of time at the farm of Sam Baker, between Bond Switch (present Onapa) and Texanna, and caged meals at the home of Willis Brooks, Baker's brother-in-law, in the Dogtown settlement west of Eufaula. Baker and Brooks (gun-fighters, feudists, and sometimes possemen) were former residents of Cooke County, Texas, where they had befriended West when he was a spindle-legged waif washing dishes in a greasy-spoon restaurant at Decatur. This was before West was employed as a horse wrangler by Texas cattleman Oscar Halsell in the early 1880s, when Halsell drove his heads from the northwest of Fort Worth and established his first ranch in Oklahoma.

During his years with the Doolin gang, West had kept in touch with Brooks and Baker. He was an occasional visitor at the Spike S ranch, and saw potential gang-member material in Al and Frank Jennings. The O'Malleys were recruited, and the gang was formed, with West as the leader.[1]

Ledbetter's first notice of the gang's formation was in mid-June 1897, when he and Tolbert investigated the robbery of a store and post office at Foyil, on the Frisco railroad southwest of Vinita. Al Jennings called it "an experimental job"; he and Frank had been furnished a "set screw" used for twisting the lock from a safe; they had robbed the post office of $700 to "pay expenses" and "just to see how the screw worked."[2] The postmaster identified Al as the man wearing a false mustache and goatee, who had cased his store the afternoon before the robbery. Tolbert obtained a commissioners warrant for Al, and took it from there.

"I was in pursuit for some time in July," Bud said. "Never did get information on Al Jennings and the other boys with him staying at one place over three or four days at a time, and that was at the mouth of the Little Spavinaw [below Salina, Cherokee Nation]."[3]

Shortly after midnight, August 16, the gang held up the southbound Santa Fe passenger train at Edmond, north of Oklahoma City. Two robbers concealed themselves behind the water tank until the train was ready to pull out, then boarded the blind baggage, climbed over the tender, covered the engineer with six-shooters, and ordered him to run the train down the track three miles where the others waited with their horses. While part of the gang kept the train crew and passengers inside the coaches with continual fire from their Winchesters, the others forced messenger W. H. May to open the express car. Two attempts to blow open the Wells-Fargo safe with dynamite failed, and West fled with his inexperienced followers back to the Creek Nation. Posses lost their trail in the Kickapoo country, but warrants were issued in Oklahoma Territory.

The gang holed up in the Dogtown area. Willis Brooks fed the O'Malleys, and Al and Frank took meals with Sam Baker. West visited his Indian sweetheart near Old Watsonville. After a few days of restlessness, and broke, they gathered at the Indian woman's cabin and plotted to rob the Katy train just south of Bond Switch. Some railroad ties stacked alongside the track were piled on the rails and set afire as the train was heard approaching. The engineer, who had been piloting locomotives in the Territory for some time, knew immediately what was in store when he spied the obstruction. He pulled the throttle open; the iron giant plowed through the heavy timbers, scattering them over the right-of-way like matchsticks; and the would-be bandits watched the train disappear into the night.

Ledbetter was soon poking around the site. "The latter part of August, I made a trip after the gang," he said. "Went 25 or 30 miles out east of Checotah . . . afterwards learned they had been seen at Barren Fork . . . hunted there on that information two, three, four days. I next got information they were in the Concharty Mountains. I was out there four, five, or six days. . . ." By the last of September, signs pointed to Baker's farm. Baker admitted that the gang had been there. Bud reminded him of the penalty for harboring federal fugitives, and Baker agreed to notify him should the outlaws reappear in the vicinity. Bud returned to Muskogee on October 2. "When I got back, I noticed in the papers that they had held up the train at Chickasha . . . ."[4]

Frustrated by their attempts on the Santa Fe at Edmond and the Katy at Bond Switch, the gang had gone west along the South Canadian to tackle the Rock Island railroad on the western border of the Chickasaw Nation. Somehow, Al Jennings had learned that $90,000 was to be expressed on the Rock Island to Fort Worth banks on October 1. He also knew that guards rode the train from El Reno to Chickasha, but none were carried on the day trains, as it was supposed bandits were not nervy enough to pull a daylight holdup. The site selected was on a high prairie eleven miles north of Chickasha, where the only human signs were the track, a section house, and some section hands at work on a siding (present Pocasset). Shortly after 11:00 A.M., the gang swooped down on the workmen and ordered them to flag the train.

A bungled job followed, as usual. Morris O'Malley took charge of the fireman and engineer. Pat O'Malley and Frank Jennings ordered the conductor and all passengers outside to stand with their backs to the coaches. Al and Little Dick West entered the express car. There was a small safe and a large safe that was billed through to Fort Worth. The messenger did not know the combination to either, as was express company policy. Al had brought along some dynamite, though he was no more experienced in the use of it than he had been at Edmond. He placed it on the large safe, and helped West lift the small safe on top of it. Al lighted the fuse, and they leaped outside. The blast ripped the side out of the express car, catapulting the small safe into the grade ditch without denting it, and leaving the large safe unharmed in the wreckage. Al and West then entered the mail car and rifled the registered letters and packages. Finding nothing they wanted, they rejoined the rest of the gang going down the line of passengers. After collecting contributions netting $300 in cash and the conductor's silver watch, all fled in an easterly direction.

A posse from Chickasha set out in direct pursuit, the robbers two hours ahead of them. Other posses came down the Santa Fe railroad from Purcell and Lexington to cover crossings on the South Canadian; a special train from Guthrie, carrying another posse, was transferred at Oklahoma City to the Choctaw line for Shawnee to intercept the gang should they successfully re-enter the Pottawatomie country; and all roads and bridges were watched day and night—without finding a trace of the outlaws.

Ledbetter, believing the gang would eventually return to their Dogtown sanctuary, contacted Sam Baker and Willis Brooks. Again, Baker promised to get word to Bud the moment the outlaws reappeared, and Brooks agreed to cooperate, reluctantly. On October 29, with no word from Brooks or Baker, Bud had left the matter in the hands of Tolbert and gone on the trail of rapist K. B. Brooks.

The gang had doubled back west through the Wichita reservation, north into Canadian County, and found refuge with a Jennings family acquaintance. They divided the loot and rested, then drifted northeast to a dugout once used by the Doolin gang on Cottonwood Creek southwest of Guthrie. Little Dick West could not help comparing his disgruntled, poorly clad cronies with his former companions of the dashing Doolin outfit. Excepting the robbery at Foyil, they had operated nearly two months, netting barely $60 each and a silver watch. One chilly evening in mid-October, West saddled his horse and rode off without an excuse or a word of comment. He briefly revisited his Indian sweetheart near Old Watsonville, learned that the gang was to be "set-up" by Brooks and Baker, and hied himself back to Cottonwood Creek. But the Jennings and O'Malley brothers had departed, and he never saw them again. He hired out as a farmhand on the Ed Fitzgerald place nearby, under an assumed name, where he was located and slain a few months later by a marshal's posse from Guthrie.

The Jennings and O'Malley brothers had wandered from Cottonwood Creek eastward along the Cimarron, riding at night and camping in secluded places in the daytime. The weather turned bitterly cold, their garments were thin and tattered. About 2:00 on the morning of October 29, they dismounted in front of Lee Nutter's general store in Cushing, Payne County. Al aroused the proprietor, telling him they wanted burial clothes for a man who had died. When Nutter opened the door, the gang rushed inside, covering him with six-shooters. They took $15, Nutter's gold watch, revolver and Winchester shotgun, the best hats, gloves, and overcoats which the establishment afforded, and rode off with a jug of whiskey and eating some stolen bananas. A posse pursued them eastward, but lost the trail in the hills near Kellyville, Creek Nation.

Ledbetter returned to Muskogee with rapist K. B. Brooks to learn that the Jennings gang was back in the Northern District. The district held two warrants against them—the one for the Foyil post office robbery, the other issued by Commissioner Robert L. McClure for the attempted holdup at Bond Switch. "The newspapers were full of reports of the other train robberies, and heavy rewards were being offered totalling $2,000." Marshal Bennett ordered Bud and Tolbert: "Go after them and get them, alive if possible—if not, get them anyway."[5]

Chapter 11

The Trail Ends at Carr Creek

IT WAS NO LONGER custom in the Indian nations to harbor and protect federal fugitives, due to the harsh consequences—not to mention the possibility of sharing in rewards. Tulsa Deputy Marshals Lon Lewis and Joe Thompson were informed that the Jennings gang had been sighted heading in the direction of Claremore. A blacksmith eight miles north of Tulsa had reset a shoe on one of their horses, and recognized the animal as one he had shod for the Spike S ranch. Ledbetter and Tolbert learned that the gang had turned south off the Claremore road to a ford on the Arkansas. On the cold, windy night of November 29, Ledbetter, Tolbert, Lewis, and Joe Thompson, with Gus Thompson, John McClanahan, and Jake Elliott as possemen, converged on the Harless ranch.[1]

John Harless, in jail at Muskogee on a "brand changing" charge, had left his wife to manage the Spike S. The house was a two-story clapboard affair—a bedroom upstairs and three rooms below. It stood in total darkness, indicating that the occupants had retired.

The officers took their positions: Tolbert north of the house behind the stone chimney of a cabin that had burned in the past; Joe Thompson and his son Gus in a point of timber to the northwest; Ledbetter and McClanahan in the barn, 200 yards to the northeast, where several horses were tied; Lon Lewis and Jake Elliott behind a stone fence south of the barn near the ranch cemetery, commanding about fifty yards of open space between the south side of the house and a peach orchard.

A wagon stood in front of the barn. Bud crept behind it to obtain a closer view of the house, and discovered Morris O'Malley, who had been posted as a lookout, asleep in his bed. Bud clamped a big hand over the neglectful sentry's mouth, disarmed him, and ushered him into the barn. With a bit of encouragement, O'Malley named the house occupants: Mrs. Harless; her younger brother, Clarence Enscoe; her hired girl, Ida Hurst; Pat O'Malley, and Al and Frank Jennings. Morris O'Malley was expertly trussed and gagged, and stretched in a stall.

The remainder of the night, the officers waited. The icy wind, sweeping sand and dust that obscured the building subsided toward morning. November 30 dawned bright and clear. Clarence Enscoe came out for a bucket of water, "evidently suspecting nothing as he was unarmed." Not seeing Morris O'Malley in the wagon, he entered the barn. Bud and McClanahan seized him, bound him, and placed him in the stall beside O'Malley.

Shortly, the hired girl appeared on the porch, called "Breakfast!" then, shivering from the cold, hurried back inside.

Enscoe's continued absence brought results. Mrs. Harless popped out of the house and came to the barn to see what was delaying her brother. Confronted by Ledbetter, she had no choice except to listen to his instructions: "Tell the Jennings bunch they are surrounded. We have fugitive warrants for them, which means they can surrender or die. You and your hired girl must get out if you want to keep away from bullets."

Mrs. Harless returned with the message. Bud heard voices "raised in argument . . . and demonstrations as if preparations were being made for resistance." Suddenly, Mrs. Harless and her hired girl, wrapped in blankets, left the house, and told Bud: "One of the men wanted to give up, but the red-headed one said, 'If the law wants a fight they can get it,' and all went upstairs and got their Winchesters." To the credit of Al Jennings, he made no attempt to hold the women as hostages.

Mrs. Harless and Ida Hurst ran to safety behind the cemetery fence. Bud made for the burned cabin to join Tolbert. As he
scuttled behind the chimney, Al Jennings fired from a window,
the bullet showering rock and mortar in his face. All the officers
"responded," and "lead flew in both directions, thick and fast."

Clapboards splintered under the onslaught. The bark of
rifles and six-shooters echoed to the rattle of kitchen utensils and
crash of crockery dissolved into shards of earthenware. The outlaws "returned fire from a heavy breastwork of furniture and
doors." Frank Jennings' clothing was "literally shot from his
back, without inflicting a single wound." Pat O'Malley received
flesh wounds in the side and on one leg. A steel-jacketed .32 caliber bullet from Ledbetter's rifle ricocheted off the iron heating
stove and lodged in Al's right leg above the knee. Bud estimated
that "60 to 100 rounds were fired." Al Jennings claimed "about
400."

As the battle progressed, the officers worked toward the
front of the house, from which most of the firing emanated. This
allowed the outlaws to slip out a back window. Unable to reach
the barn and their horses, they fled through the orchard into
the bottoms of Snake Creek.

It was several minutes before Bud learned they had
escaped, and some of the possemen claimed later that "his
string of vitriolic curses that filled the air were too warm to be
recorded."

The officers searched the bottoms, but lost the trail in the
icy waters of the creek. Morris O'Malley and the gang's horses
and saddles were taken to Muskogee.[2]

The fugitives had come upon two Euchee Indian boys in a
wagon. They commandeered them and their outfit, drove past
Okmulgee during the night, and hid in the brush all the next
day. That night, Frank Jennings tried to drive them toward Oklahoma Territory, hoping to reach an old family acquaintance in
Canadian County, but lost his way. They turned back to the
North Canadian, released the Indian boys at daylight, and proceeded to the home of Willis Brooks.

With Little Dick West no longer part of the outfit, Brooks
had no interest in their plight, and shuttled them to Sam Baker.
By that time, Al Jennings and Pat O'Malley were "suffering so

severely from their wounds" that Baker insisted on going to Checotah for a "friendly" doctor. The wounds were "cared for as best possible," and Baker furnished a team and straw-filled wagon to take the trio eastward to the Arkansas border. Baker didn't tell them that, while in Checotah, he had complied with his promise to Ledbetter, allegedly in return for Bud's promise to share any rewards received for the gang's capture.

The three outlaws left Baker's farm at 3:00 the morning of December 6. Al Jennings and Pat O'Malley were wrapped in blankets and concealed beneath the straw in the wagon. Frank Jennings was driving.

Eight miles southeast, the road passed through a deep cut sloping down to the ford on Carr Creek. Ledbetter and Tolbert, with two possemen, had reached the ford shortly after midnight. They felled a tree and laid it across the road well into the cut. Tolbert and the possemen stationed themselves atop the high banks on each side; Ledbetter crouched in the branches of the fallen tree.

The wagon came jolting and rattling down the frozen road. As the team reared to a stop at the barricade, Bud called out: "Throw away your guns or be killed!"

Frank Jennings recognized the big lawman's voice, saw the leveled Winchester boring into his flushed face in the moonlight, and complied without hesitation. Al Jennings and Pat O'Malley popped from under the straw and promptly put up their hands as the other officers sprang into sight. By evening, the trio had joined Morris O'Malley in the Muskogee jail.[3]

The *Phoenix* congratulated Bud and Tolbert on "landing the gang. . . . They will receive some substantial benefit for their successful work."[4] But what portion, if any, of the $2,000 they received was never mentioned by the deputies nor by the press, and all Sam Baker got out of betraying the Jennings gang was "a good laugh."[5]

A couple of years later, Baker became city marshal of Checotah, and killed four men while wearing the badge. Jackson Thompson, who lived in Checotah during the period, recalled Sam's demise: "One night he got drunk and [Deputy U.S. Marshal] Jones ordered him home. . . . Instead of doing what he was told, Sam reached for his gun. Jones was quicker . . . sent a bullet through Sam. Jones took Baker's gun and laid him down on the floor. 'Don't shoot me any more, you have killed me,' Baker said . . . After quite some time, Baker recovered . . . and was killed on the street one afternoon by Will Torens [a school boy, Will Torrence]."[6]

The Jennings gang conducted themselves as "model prisoners" after their capture, and on December 25, Bud and Tolbert sent Christmas dinner for them to the Muskogee jail—to which all four members responded:

> Messrs. Tolbert and Ledbetter,
> Dear Sirs and Friends:
>   Dr. Bennett, USM, and Mr. Lubbes, jailer have kindly delivered to us the excellent Christmas dinner presented by yourselves, which proves you to be connisseurs as well as men of big hearts and Christmas spirits. We know not if you have any profession of faith, or to what creed you adhere, if any, but we realize that you are Christians at heart.
>   Therefore, accept our sincere thanks for your generous offer of dinner.
>
> Sincerely,
Pat and Morris O'Malley
Al and Frank Jennings [7]

Morris O'Malley "wasn't hurt much from his wounds . . . was all right in a few days." But the ball in Al Jennings' leg was "giving him much trouble," and Monday afternoon, February 22, a large number of business and professional men gathered at the Fite & Blakemore hospital to witness the first use of x-ray in Indian Territory:

> Doctors [F. B.] Fite, [J. L.] Blakemore, Thompson and Reeves were all present and each had more or less of the work in charge, while Mr. Moody had charge of the electrical machinery.
>   Jennings climbed upon the table and told Jailer Lubbes "if that thing electrocuted him, he (Lubbes) was to be held accountable." Jennings was as much interested in the scientific side of the question as of the purely personal feature of the test.
>   With drawn curtains the experiment began. The electrical apparatus kept up a terrific rattle, much like the click of a sewing machine, though much louder, and the glass bulb filled

with a greenish, milky light. Jennings' leg was placed near the bulb and then the operator put a funnel-like box (called the fluroscope) on the opposite side, put his eye at the spout and looked. The bullet was soon located and everybody in the room given an opportunity to see it for themselves. Later, a sensitized plate was placed where the fluroscope had been and a good photograph made of the bullet and its location.

Owing to the time consumed it was thought best to delay the operation until the next day, as the patient had gone through considerable strain. . . .[8]

Jennings was returned to the hospital Tuesday afternoon. A second examination was made, then he was put under an anaesthetic:

So perfect had the location been made that Dr. Fite cut straight down through almost two inches of muscle and touched the bullet at the bottom of the cut. With a pair of forcepts the bullet and some patches of cloth were quickly removed, the wound was then dressed and Jennings rallied all right from the influence of the drug.

The bullet proved to be a part of the lead tip of a 32 steel bullet, and those who knew the circumstances of the fight say it was undoubtedly put there by Deputy Bud Ledbetter.[9]

Bud regretted missing the operation. In mid-February, he had received a tip on the whereabouts of Joe Crowell, a member of the Crowell gang that for some time had "figured prominently in the federal courts of the country." Crowell had escaped at Muskogee while being held for Missouri authorities on indictments for robbery, larceny, and assault to kill. Two of his brothers were serving time in the penitentiary. A third brother was in a Missouri jail awaiting trial for highway robbery. The morning of February 22, Bud rode up to Crowell's shack on the Arkansas, south of Tulsa. "Crowell saw him coming and escaping from the house made for the brush. Ledbetter followed . . . called to him to halt or take the consequences." Crowell "paid no attention to the deputy's command," threw a shot at Bud, and "continued to run, when the officer fired one shot with deadly effect."[10]

Bud was in Muskogee, adjusting matters with Missouri authorities in the Crowell case, when a man named Allen Clay was landed in the federal bastille "to board at government expense." While serving process on Clay, at Vinita, Paden Tolbert hadn't fared well. "He was struck over the head with a pistol by Clay and his skull mashed in. The physicians removed a piece of the skull about the size of a silver dollar, and Tolbert seems to be a little inconvenienced by the serious wound. Clay was arrested immediately after the assault."[11]

Tolbert recovered sufficiently to testify with many other witnesses at the Jennings gang's trials at Muskogee during the April-May 1898 term of district court. In the Foyil post office robbery, the gang "proved an alibi; the government failed to make a case, it's main witness [the postmaster] having died"; and Judge Springer "instructed the jury to bring in a verdict of not guilty, which they did without leaving the box." However, all four defendants were held under bond of $5,000 each for robbing the U.S. mails in the Southern District during the Rock Island holdup near Chickasha.[12]

Al Jennings faced a separate charge for "assault with intent to kill James Franklin Ledbetter" during the battle at the Spike S ranch. He was found guilty on May 31, "the jury being out only three hours," and sentenced to five years, at hard labor in the penitentiary at Fort Leavenworth. Al moved for a new trial; the motion was "overruled, exceptions saved, and the case regularly appealed to the U.S. Court of Appeals for the Indian Territory." The judgment of the Muskogee court was affirmed, Judge William H. H. Clayton of the Central District writing the opinion, and concurred by Judge Hosea Townsend of the Southern District and supernumerary Judge Thomas.[13]

Pending the appeal, the Jennings and O'Malley brothers were delivered to U.S. Marshal Hammer of the Southern District and held at Ardmore until February 1899, when they were tried before Judge Townsend and convicted for the mail robbery at Chickasha. Frank Jennings and the O'Malleys were given five- year terms at Fort Leavenworth. A trainman had been mortally injured in the express car blast, and Al, as leader of the train bandits, was sentenced to the penitentiary at Columbus, Ohio, for life.[14]

In 1900, through the persistent efforts of Al's brother John and Judge Amos Ewing of Kingfisher, President McKinley commuted Al's life sentence to "imprisonment for five years, with all allowances for good conduct." With these allowances, his term would have expired June 20, 1902; but a few days prior to this date the U.S. attorney for the Northern District ordered him transferred from the Ohio prison to Fort Leavenworth. Jennings filed for a writ of habeas corpus in the U.S. Circuit Court for the Eastern District of Missouri, at St. Louis. The circuit court held that the marshal of the Northern District had acted without authority of law in surrendering petitioner to the custody of the marshal of the Southern District after judgment and sentence had been pronounced committing him to the Leavenworth prison, "thereby postponing the execution of the first sentence indefinitely"; that due to these circumstances, the prisoner had been in "actual custody, undergoing imprisonment, since June 4, 1898"—in jail at Ardmore, in the Ohio penitentiary, and a small portion of the time at Leavenworth. Deducting the allowance for good behavior as prescribed by federal statute, his term would have expired prior to the date of application for the writ of habeas corpus.[15]

Jennings was discharged from prison on November 13, 1902, and returned to Oklahoma Territory. Ledbetter would hear much more of this comic-opera ex-bandit.

During the April-May 1898 trials of the Jennings gang at Muskogee, Bud was also a chief witness in the K. B. Brooks rape case. Brooks was tried before Judge Thomas, found guilty on April 29, and sentenced "to be hanged by the neck until dead."

It was the second death sentence passed by Judge Thomas. At Wagoner, on December 2, 1897, Henry Whitefield, a black employee of the Katy railroad, had ambushed and killed one George Miller over a young laundress, Nancy Adkins, with whom he was infatuated. Whitefield had been convicted and sentenced on April 2, 1898.

Judge Thomas set the execution of Brooks and Whitefield for July 1.

A barn-like gallows was erected in the stockade at the north end of the jail yard. "Shortly after 8:00 A.M. the men were dressed in suits of black, white shirts and slippers. . . . The night before, two coffins in which the criminals were to be buried were placed upright in the lower portion of the gallows. . . . Hundreds of people surrounded the stockade, but only ten passes, besides those for the jail officials were issued by Marshal Bennett.

"At nine o'clock, Marshal Bennett read the death warrants while both men listened attentively. Brooks handed out a photograph [of himself] and requested it be sent to his people at Paris, Texas." At 9:17 the two men stepped on the trap door, "where Marshal Bennett, Jailer Lubbes, Turnkey Wilkerson, and Judge Barker [Deputy Marshal William F. Barker, ex-judge of a Cherokee court] were waiting with Father Charles and two colored ministers. They shook hands with the condemned men and bid them good-bye, after which their feet and hands were tied and songs and prayers offered for their souls. . . . Judge Barker sprang the trap at 9:32 o'clock. The necks of both men were broken." They were pronounced dead by Doctors Fite and Blakemore. "The bodies were placed in coffins, taken to the colored Baptist church, where funeral services were held, and buried in the colored cemetery near town. . . .

"This was the first hanging in Indian Territory since its - removal from the jurisdiction of the Western District of - Arkansas."[16]

Though the press touted Brooks' case as "a big feather in Ledbetter's cap," Bud considered the capture of the Jennings gang his "most difficult trail" and the "highlight" of his first four years as a lawman in the Cherokee and Creek nations.[17]

Chapter 12

"Hop-Ale" Raids and a "Brush Court" Expedition

In MID-1898, LEDBETTER'S service was needed in another major event, which was without gunfire but no less hectic.

During 1897, the national press had aroused public sympathy for the insurrection in Cuba over the issue of independence and called on leading politicians in Congress to pressure both outgoing President Cleveland and incoming President McKinley to take a stand against the atrocities committed and the concentration camps set up by the Spanish colonial authorities. On February 17, 1898, the U.S. battleship *Maine* was sunk in Havana harbor, killing 260 of its 350 crew members. The nation united in belief in the culpability of Spain, and the cry "Remember the Maine," like "Remember the Alamo," became a patriot's call to action. War was formally declared on April 25. Congress also provided for a larger army, with cavalry regiments to be recruited in the Rocky Mountain and Southwest regions, and Col. Leonard Wood, with Theodore Roosevelt as lieutenant colonel, began organization of the First U.S. Volunteer Cavalry, to become known as "Roosevelt's Rough Riders."

In the midst of the Jennings gang and Brooks trials at Muskogee, Secretary of War Russell A. Alger telegraphed Judge Springer and Judge Thomas that "175 picked men, good shots and good riders," were wanted from Indian Territory for Colonel Wood's regiment, and asked: "When can you have them ready for muster and where?" Springer and Thomas replied: "Can furnish men by middle of next week . . . Muskogee best place for examination and muster." Thomas telegraphed Judge Clayton and Judge Townsend of the Central and Southern districts, and Townsend replied: "Can furnish 50 or whole 175 if desired." At Vinita, Deputy Marshal White promptly enlisted "100 Indian Territory sharpshooters," with himself as captain, and reported them "ready on call."[1]

First Lt. Allyn K. Capron, Seventh U.S. Cavalry at Fort Sill, arrived at Muskogee on May 6 to screen and register the applicants. Dr. Fite served as medical examiner. Those accepted were housed in the Women's Christian Temperance Union building on the east side of town and slept upstairs on the hay-strewn floor. "An immense throng of eager citizens and visitors surrounded the building just east of the post office where the work was being carried on." In the opera house that evening, "in the presence of the wildly excited crowd," Judge Thomas "passed sentence" on the entire Spanish navy and condemned it to "everlasting defeat."[2]

Muskogee belatedly received the report of the crushing defeat administered to Spain's squadron at Manila on May 1 by Commodore George Dewey, operating from his Pacific base in Hong Kong. "Never before in the history of the city was there such a tremendous and spontaneous outburst of patriotism as was witnessed Saturday night [May 7] on the streets. From early morn till eventide little crowds of people gathered to exchange congratulations on the supremacy of American arms in the Orient. The enthusiasm increased . . . till it was decided to celebrate the great naval victory in a befitting manner. About a hundred railroad men, assisted by equally as many Muskogee citizens, prepared a big bonfire on the vacant space south of Hotel Adams. . . ."[3]

Ledbetter headed a "squad" of officers assigned to "maintain order as necessary." The celebrants "formed themselves in a marching brigade with abundant red fire to escort Judge Thomas from the court house to the scene of the demonstration to address them on the occasion. Soon the square was filled with a swarming, howling mass of humanity." Torpedoes roared and fireworks exploded. As Judge Thomas mounted the platform, "cheers rent the air . . . women waved their handkerchiefs and shouted . . . staid old citizens threw up their hands and danced with joy." Judge Thomas ably entertained the crowd with an hour-long address regarding the nation's defense and the men who controlled its destiny. His remarks were frequently interrupted by applause, and when he concluded, "the climax of applause was reached. Not until a late hour did the crowd disperse, with the thought of a continued revenge on 'Maine' that would terminate in the presentation to Cuba of a flag upon which shall be emblazoned freedom and liberty." The Ledbetter "squad" worked throughout the night, protecting against sharpers and gamblers who invariably exploited such gatherings, and policing the "hop-ale" joints that "supplied the needs of the thirsty."[4]

Seventy-five applicants from the Muskogee area and "100 more from Ardmore, Sapulpa and Tulsa" were accepted to form troops "A" and "B"—Troop "A" in charge of Lieutenant Capron, assisted by Lt. John R. Thomas, Jr. (Judge Thomas' son); Troop "B" in charge of Capt. Peter R. Bruce, assisted by Lt. F. E. Nichols. The evening of May 13 the troops were "tendered a parting lunch" by 2,000 citizens assembled at the fairgrounds. "After lunch, each soldier was presented with a buttonhole boquet by the young ladies present, then they gathered about the bandstand and rent the air with cheers as the strains of 'Dixie' floated from Masek's band." The master of ceremonies, Gen. Pleasant Porter, Chief of the Creek Nation, was "en rapport with the soldiers . . . his very appearance welcomed with prolonged manifestations of pleasure. . . . General Porter was followed by Judge Springer, and the rounding out of his sentences were answered from the army with about all their available lung power."[5]

Sunday, May 15, was "another feverish day," with Ledbetter and his "squad" again in evidence. At 9:00 A.M., the troops were marched to the Katy depot to answer roll call and have administered for the third time the mustering oath of allegiance for a term of two years. They were served breakfast "in the old army fashion," thus reminding them of "the bill of fare they would share for a while, at least." Throughout the day, the platforms and grounds swarmed with people exchanging good wishes and tokens of love and affection. "The band came down and rendered several cheering selections." Finally, the troops were ordered aboard, and the train departed for San Antonio, Texas, "profusely decorated with the emblematic colors of the United States, along with a gorgeous banner which read, 'We are going to right a wrong, Indian Territory Rough Riders.'"[6]

The Muskogee recruits were given a brief period of training at San Antonio, redesignated as Rough Rider troops "L" and "M," and embarked to Cuba under the leadership of Roosevelt. Their many heroic and self-sacrificing deeds before Santiago, at El Caney and San Juan Hill, and the eventual surrender of Spanish forces on August 13, is a matter of history. Because Judge Thomas had been "untiring in arranging and looking after details connected with the formation of Troops A and B," Secretary of War Alger named him the "war governor" for Indian Territory. Deputy Marshal White was "deserving of much praise" for organizing the sharpshooters at Vinita, many of whom had enlisted with the Muskogee companies, and Ledbetter and his squad were lauded for maintaining order.[7]

The work of the Ledbetter squad was not finished, however.

In a "malt tonic decision" of mid-April, Judge Springer had noted the "inability" of the district judges and U.S. commissioners to deal with "gambling, drunkenness, fighting, carrying concealed weapons and many other misdemeanors" being committed "so extensively" in the very shadows of the courts; that "because these minor crimes are but stepping stones to graver ones, the lamentable situation for handling and curbing these miscreants and hoodlums becomes all the more apparent and the anxiety for a change that will provide proper means for trial and punishment of such offenders all the more serious." The *Phoenix* observed: "The truth of the matter is that prohibition does not prohibit. . . . Whether the saloon is open in the background the demand will be supplied . . . As long as red liquor and 'white mule' command a price there will be those who will engage in the traffic."[8]

Judge Thomas "minced no words" in his charge to the grand jury in May—"hop-ale joints are a curse and a disgrace to any community . . . those who persist in violating the law should be prosecuted to the fullest extent and the most severe penalties imposed."[9]

Immediately following the departure of the troops for San Antonio on May 16, the Ledbetter squad raided the hop-ale joints of Muskogee. "The general roundup of the tough element and gamblers netted a few dozen more boarders for the federal jail."[10] Indictments found by the grand jury "were many and as a result the town is rid of an army of petty gamblers, dive keepers and inmates. This upheaval is purifying, for the time at least."[11]

By act of Congress (Curtis Bill) June 28, 1898, the trial and punishment of "minor crimes," as defined by Judge Springer, became more or less a local responsibility. The first interests of the Dawes Commission in negotiating with the Indian tribes for the allotment of their lands in the severalty and the eventual dissolution of their national governments had been the anomalous condition under which Indian Territory towns of considerable size and importance existed. Tribal agreements had provided for segregation from allotment all townsite acreages and the survey, appraisal, and sale of lots to owners of improvements thereon, and sale by auction of all surplus lots to the highest bidder. The Curtis Bill allowed towns of 200 or more inhabitants to incorporate and pass ordinances against misdemeanors, particularly the sale or introduction of intoxicants, though the latter remained a federal offense.[12]

Accordingly, many towns filed petitions with plats of their proposed municipalities and received decrees from the U.S. courts to incorporate. By September, the first officials of Muskogee had been elected for one-year terms, sworn in by Judge Springer, and the city was off and running with ordinances covering everything from the operation of local businesses to regulating the conduct of its citizens, with a city attorney and city marshal to enforce the same.

The Curtis Bill also gave fresh impetus to railroad building. Several branch lines were already under construction or had been completed to developing centers in the Choctaw and Chickasaw nations. In the Creek Nation, the Frisco began extending its track from Sapulpa to Okmulgee, from Sapulpa south-westward through Kellyville and the tent-and-shack town of Bristow, and toward Chandler and Oklahoma City,

Oklahoma Territory. There was a great deal of trouble from those seeking to profit in every nefarious way in and around the construction camps. Crimes ranged from misdemeanors to murder.

According to Harry H. Adams, federal court bailiff under Marshal Bennett in 1898, "Muskogee was the closest court and the aggrieved parties [along the Frisco] declined to travel that distance to secure a warrant for the arrest of the offending parties. They would take the matter in their own hands, which in many cases resulted in killing. It seemed impossible to bring the troubles to Muskogee. As conditions grew from bad to worse, Marshal Bennett obtained permission from the attorney general in Washington to establish a traveling court, called a 'Brush Court' because of its transient and various locations."[13]

The caravan consisted of two covered wagons carrying bedding, canned goods and staples, cooking utensils, folding chairs, and tents for camping and holding court; a wagon for transporting prisoners; hacks and buggies to be used by the court officials; and saddle horses for the deputy marshals. The personnel consisted of U.S. Commissioner Dave Yancey, as presiding judge; Harry Adams to assist with court proceedings; Marshal Bennett and Deputies Ledbetter, Lon Lewis, William Barker, and Dave Adams (father of Harry Adams); a black teamster; and a black cook named Bill Wright. Interpreters were to be picked up at court settings, as needed.

Harry Adams detailed the expedition, as follows:

> We left Muskogee in August . . . took a westerly direction and after a hard day's travel camped the first night on Mountain Creek near the old Spike S ranch. The next day we proceeded to Polecat Creek . . . made camp near Sapulpa, from where we had been receiving many complaints of law violations. The officers made a raid in Sapulpa . . . . cleaning out several questionable places and gambling joints and making several arrests. No trials were held there as all parties made bond. . . .
>
> Our next stop was just west of Kellyville where we camped three days while the officers were scouting the vicinity . . . waiting for a big stomp dance that was to take place at the old Tuskegee stomp ground on the Little Deep Fork southeast of Bris-

tow. Breaking camp, we made it to Tiger Jack's [Euchee Indian scout and trailer] south of Kellyville that evening and spent the night. Starting the next morning we made it to Jesse Allen's ranch southeast of Bristow for dinner. Leaving Jesse's ranch we proceeded to a place near the Tuskegee stomp ground, arriving late in the afternoon and making camp about three-quarters of a mile from the ground on the opposite bank of Little Deep Fork.

Outposts were immediately established. During the evening each straggling Indian who approached the camp was taken into custody or detained . . . to prevent them informing others of our presence. . . . That night we made a raid on the stomp ground and due to a complete surprise the raid . . . resulted in the arrest of nine people for whom we had warrants. The next day we held court in camp . . . all prisoners who were found guilty were bound over, and due to the lack of facilities for confining the prisoners, we would shackle them and chain them to trees and tent posts.

We were in that camp five days and the posse was busy scouring that part of the country for parties we had warrants for . . . occasionally bringing in others for trial.

A gang led by three brothers named Hughes had been giving trouble in that vicinity for some time. About three o'clock one morning Bud Ledbetter, Lon Lewis, Jesse Allen [Creek lighthorseman and deputy marshal] and Tiger Jack left camp on their trail. . . . Between daylight and sunup the officers contacted the gang coming in from one of their raids. The officers commanded their arrest which immediately resulted in a gun battle and the death of one of the Hughes brothers. Another brother was brought in by Jesse Allen and later in the day Bud Ledbetter and Lon Lewis came in together with another member of the gang. . . .

After the general cleanup of the vicinity of Little Deep Fork we broke camp and proceeded to Bristow. . . . The Frisco track was not yet completed into Bristow. As our caravan approached from the south, there was an exodus of gamblers, bootleggers and general riff-raff from the north side of town. We made camp on the east side of the right-of-way . . . raided the place immediately upon our arrival, not missing a tent or shack, making three arrests and capturing many gambling devices of various descriptions, of which we built several bonfires at different places in the one street of the town. The next day we held court, and at the same time made a raid on a construction gang that was building the track. . . . When the posse approached about half of the gang fled to the brush, however they made two or three arrests. The next day the posse adopted greater strategy . . . surrounded the camp from all sides not permitting escape in any direction. . . . Three more arrests were made, including one negro wanted for murder, who was later tried and sentenced to Fort Leavenworth for life. . . . We had about thirty prisoners all chained to trees. . . . [While] we were in camp at Bristow the only one of the Hughes brothers that had escaped in the gun battle near Tuskegee came to contact his brother who was there as a prisoner, which resulted in his arrest. . . . We were compelled to hire another team and wagon for transportation of the large number of prisoners we had collected.

Leaving Bristow we proceeded in the direction of old Mounds, camping that night on Polecat Creek. . . . Incidentally that night was the first and only rain we experienced during that expedition, and the only inconvenience it caused was that we had to chain the prisoners in the tents. . . . Breaking camp early the next morning we experienced a slow and tedious trip over rough and muddy road or trail until late in the afternoon we reached old Mounds . . . camped there that night and after another days journey we arrived at Buford Miller's ranch on Duck Creek about fifteen miles west and a little south of where the town of Haskell now stands.

We were in camp there about three days, during which two wagons with the necessary guards took the prisoners to Muskogee. As soon as the wagons and guards returned we broke camp and moved to Okmulgee, where we . . . established our camp on the little creek north of town and spent five days . . . raiding and closing up several places of vice, whiskey and gambling joints and making several arrests . . .

After cleaning out Okmulgee we broke camp and started for Muskogee, the mission of the Brush Court completed.[14]

Recent alterations at the Muskogee jail enabled Marshal Bennett to accommodate the aggregation of new prisoners. In February 1898 the attorney general had recommended to Congress "the propriety of appropriation" to improve the jails at Muskogee, South McAlester, and Ardmore and the "holding" places at other court towns "to provide sanitation, proper warmth and ventilation" for federal prisoners, and "to prevent constant and occasional escapes."[15] During the summer, several changes had been made at the Muskogee stockade—a building erected for use as a kitchen and storeroom; the former kitchen remodeled into hospital wards; a bathhouse in which prisoners were given "a sponge bath daily and compelled to take a hot water bath every Saturday"; a new outhouse, with the old cesspool "fixed up and fenced"; the former hospital building converted for "prison purposes"; and a 33 x 80-foot exercising space added to the jail yard.[16]

On October 4 two dozen "brush court" prisoners were taken from Muskogee "to be arraigned before the grand jury and stand trial" before Judge Thomas at Vinita for offenses ranging from "introducing and disposing of liquor and larceny to embezzlement, riot to disturb the peace, assault to rape, and murder." One convicted of larceny was given a five-year sentence and one convicted of murder was sentenced to life in the Columbus, Ohio, penitentiary. A few waived preliminary or had their sentences set aside to appear in cases later as witnesses, and were transferred back to Muskogee for trial in mid-November.[17]

After court began at Vinita, Ledbetter and other deputies raided hop-ale joints and made nine captures around Tahlequah. By year's end, the additional prison space at the Muskogee jail was filled to overflowing.

Chapter 13

Discouraged and Disenchanted

DISEASE, DISASTER AND other untoward events marked Ledbetter's career during 1899.

In February, smallpox was discovered in scattered sections of the Creek Nation, and Bud was one of several deputy marshals assigned to assist Katy railroad officials in preventing unvaccinated persons from leaving all trains running from Vinita to South McAlester. A discovery of smallpox victims in the U.S. court at Muskogee caused adjournment until the courtroom could be fumigated. The city council created a board of health composed of local physicians, admonishing all citizens to clean up their premises and, though on doubtful ground, set up a quarantine line five miles beyond the city's boundaries on all roads leading from the infected area, enforced by guards with shotguns. U.S. Indian Inspector J. George Wright vested Dr. Fite with control over the railroad and Dr. Blakemore over the country west to Okmulgee, and ordered all infected areas quarantined and pesthouses established. Houses in certain infested sections were burned to halt the spread of disease. Congress eventually appropriated $50,000 to pay for these losses, the local physicians for their services and medicine dispensed, and the guards who maintained the quarantine.

In the midst of the epidemic, Muskogee suffered a confla-

gration, which became known as the "Great Fire of 1899." The
Phoenix of February 23 reported:

> About 5:30 this morning a feeble wail of "fire" was heard,
> followed by the popping of firearms and the hoarse bellowing
> of engines in the [railroad] yard, and then all Muskogee
> assembled to make a most unequal effort to stay the destruc-
> tion. . . .
>
> The fire started from the explosion of a coal oil stove near
> Cat Fish Kelly's place, in one row of three or four small one-
> story shacks on the east side of Court Street and nearly oppo-
> site the United States court building. [It] immediately spread
> to William Mann's Hotel and south to the Times Building, and
> the fierce, biting wind drove it eastward to the rear of the
> buildings on the west side of Main Street . . . the center from
> which it spread north to and including the splendid two-story
> building of the Maddin Hardware, Co., southward including
> the new English stone block, and all the property directly east
> of these to the railroad yards. . . .
>
> The fire crossed Railroad [Broadway] Street south long
> enough to destroy the M.K.&T. freight house, the telegraph
> office, and scorch the grocery of the Patterson Mercantile Co.
> The brick building of the First National Bank and Patterson
> Mercantile Co. [corners of Main and Broadway] held the fire
> in check and prevented the loss of the remainder of the busi-
> ness portion of the town. The U.S. court building . . . the front
> rooms of which for several times were a roaring furnace . . .
> was saved.

Though one-half of the business district had been destroyed, the city's nearly 5,000 citizens were anxious to rebuild.
On February 26 a mass meeting was held, resolutions adopted,
and a committee appointed, headed by Marshal Bennett and
Gen. Pleasant Porter of the Creeks. A memorial drafted to the
Department of the Interior resulted in the appointment of a
townsite committee. The burned district was inspected, and by
the end of March, Muskogee was being relieved of its situation.

On March 29 Ledbetter came down from Vinita to assist in
maintaining order at the beginning of the largest land distribu-
tion in American history. A large frame building at the northwest corner of Second Street and Okmulgee Avenue housed the
Dawes Commission, its records, and a large force of employees.

On April 1 hundreds of Creek Indians and freedmen jammed the streets and lined up before the several clerks to indicate their holdings and receive certificates of allotment of 160 acres each.

A faction of Creek full-bloods under the leadership of Chitto "Crazy Snake" Harjo refused enrollment or to accept land parcels, declaring their determination to adhere to the old customs and assuming that the federal government would honor its ancient treaties with them. No trouble occurred at the allotting office, but some time later, seventy of the rebels were rounded up by Marshal Bennett and his deputies, assisted by a U.S. Cavalry troop from Fort Reno and a detail of Indian police. They were lodged in the Muskogee stockade and charged with seditious conspiracy and other offenses. Judge Thomas admonished them on the hopelessness of defying the government. After subscribing to an oath administered by the judge to keep the peace, they were duly enrolled in the jail bullpen and sent home. This did not end the matter. Much more would be heard of Chitto Harjo in the "Snake Uprising" a decade later.

Ledbetter was back in Muskogee as a witness in several whiskey cases in the May term of court, and heard Judge Thomas charge the grand jury: " A man who sells intoxicating liquors in Indian Territory should be indicted for every drink he sells . . . whether they sell whiskey, beer, wine, ale, hop-ale, Rochester tonic, or by whatever name it is known. Everything that produces intoxication is prohibited by law, and every man who runs a place of that kind . . . is going to be stopped if I have to summon a grand jury every week, or keep you here until the sun is hot enough to scorch the hair off your heads."[1]

Two months later, Bud accompanied Marshal Bennett on a second brush court expedition—"a general scouting tour," the press called it, "accompanied by a U.S. commissioner who would try a prisoner as soon as he was captured." The commissioner and marshals "lived in tents and practically covered the Northern District," returning to Muskogee on August 4 with forty-four culprits, most of them whiskey peddlers. During the expedition, "twenty others were arrested, examined and released."[2]

December brought another shift in the Indian Territory judiciary. Judge Springer moved to Washington as resident counsel for the Cherokee and Creek nations. President McKinley appointed as his successor Joseph A. Gill, a West Virginia native, then in law practice at Colby, Kansas. Judge Gill arrived in Muskogee on December 27, opened his first term of court two days later, and by operation of law, became a member of the court of appeals with Judges Clayton, Townsend, and Thomas.[3]

Judge Gill proved uniquely knowledgeable in all civil, criminal, and probate matters. Ledbetter, however, did not feel the support Judge Springer had given law enforcement. He thought the new judge leaned toward the idea persisting among a great segment of the populace that deputy marshals had a soft snap and were getting rich on prisoners they delivered to the courts.

The idea rankled Bud. A deputy was allowed ten cents per mile one way only and living expenses not to exceed $2 per day for each prisoner and himself. If necessary to employ a guard, he received the same. And he had to obtain receipts for everything. If he went into the wilderness, the allowance was only twenty-five cents a day, even for the coarsest kind of food, with horse feed charged in proportion. When sent in pursuit of a gang that was hitting hard and fast, before the identity of the outlaws was known and a writ issued, he got nothing and bore his own expense. Sometimes he worked a week before the issuance of writs. If a reward offered by express companies and railroads was shared or collected, he considered himself lucky.

The people expected and were entitled to prompt and efficient protection, but Bud wondered if they could justly demand that officers outlay money and time for which they did not receive a cent. Too, his children were now grown—George, twenty-four, and Dolly, twenty-two—married and making their own ways. His wife, Mary Josephine, spent days alone while field duty and the courts kept him in the saddle, though she bore his long and frequent absences admirably. Despite his desire to serve the common good and his love for the hard and dangerous work of manhunting, he was finding a deputy's life disenchanting.

Bud really became discouraged when the issue of heavy government expense of apprehending criminals in the Territory came to a head in the summer of 1900. The auditor of the Department of Justice held up more than $20,000 of accounts of the district marshals, alleging they had exceeded the amounts allowed by appropriations, and had secured from the government, illegally, more expense for their deputies than the amount of their salaries for the entire term. Unless some action was taken by Congress, more than $150,000 would be chargeable against them personally.

In turn, the comptroller of the treasury practically nullified the criminal law in the Territory by allowing deputy marshals no mileage for arrests made at places of holding court and only fifty cents for arresting a criminal in one of the remote sections of the Territory and taking him to Muskogee, a distance of 150 miles. Moreover, a deputy must pay the railroad fare of himself and prisoner to Muskogee and his own fare back to his starting point. Hack hire, which had always been allowed, and the expense of transporting prisoners to and from court, were deemed unnecessary. Witnesses were allowed only fifty cents per day and no mileage for attending court. Jurors were allowed only $1.50 for rendering a verdict, and if no verdict was rendered, they received nothing.

During January 1901, U.S. District Attorney Soper spent days in Washington, insisting that Congress attend to what he called "an outrage." Soper expressed himself in "very forcible and emphatic terms to a number of senators and representatives," and received assurances that the claims would be taken care of, "whether in this session or the next congress."[4] On February 7 Marshal Bennett was informed by the Department of Justice that the attorney general had overruled the decision of the comptroller of the treasury and that the old fees would be restored. The attorney general's action was "hailed with delight by the people of the entire Indian Territory."[5]

By this time, Bud had resigned his deputy's commission and become city marshal at Vinita.

Chapter 14

City Marshal at Vinita

FARMING AND FRUIT AND vegetable growing had extended gradually in the Cooweescowee district of the Cherokee Nation. While Vinita attributed its continued growth to being a center for disposal of these products, large numbers of range cattle were still brought in from Texas and Mexico to feed and fatten for northern and eastern markets, and the town remained headquarters for cattlemen and cowboys.

Lee Crutchfield, who sometimes served as posseman for Paden Tolbert, recalled that Ledbetter was appointed to fill an unexpired term as marshal on the promise to stop the carrying of firearms in Vinita:

"At that time a gun or two guns was the equipment of every man and no business man thought of coming to work on mornings without strapping on his six-shooter. . . . Within a week Ledbetter had stopped the gun-totin' and didn't have to shoot anyone. He simply picked out some of the toughs, knocked them out with his fists, took their guns away, and when they revived told them to go home and forget about guns. . . .

"Nobody doubted Ledbetter's own ability with a revolver. One of his favorite stunts was to set a row of tin cans on a bridge stringer near Vinita and pick them off in rapid fire fashion."[1]

The federal building in which the district judge and U.S.

91

commissioner held court stood at the northwest corner of Canadian Avenue and Wilson Street, the upper floor used for court sessions and the downstairs for offices. In back was a 100-foot square "bull pen," which Bud was allowed to use in lieu of the town's boxlike jail for recalcitrant prisoners. Compared to his federal service, his work as city marshal was quite routine— arresting drunks, quieting brawls, and breaking up crap games.

A typical example appeared in the Vinita *Indian Chieftain* of February 12, 1901:

> Whenever you see a "gentleman of color" walking with a slight limp in his off leg, and wearing a frightened look, you can be pretty well assured that he was in the crap game in an old cabin in the south end of town last Saturday night. Marshal Ledbetter heard loud talking in the shanty and approached near a window. He heard the rattle of the "bones" and the clinking of small silver coins as a voice would say, "Come on, niggers, I'll fade you." The man who tossed the dice would say, "Come on seben, fo' my baby wants a pair a shoes." All in chorus the players shouted, "Eight's the point." All then followed in a jumble of voices, "Come on eight, neber eight, it's too late, eight fo' me there dice, dere's no chops in mammy's house." The dice would finally come up seven in spite of the talking to they had received, and the marshal determined that he would "take" the whole bunch. . . . It was at that time that his presence was discovered and the players made their escape pellmell out the back way and hot-footed across the prairie running as long as they could. Bud fired a few shots in the air to hasten their flight. He has all their names and will arrest them . . . and wanted them all to commence now saving up money to pay their fines or they will have to go to jail.

In March Bud ran for a full term of office. It was a "hot" election, not only because of his "strict" enforcement policy, but due to an attempt by his opponent, a man named Gilstrap, and Gilstrap's friends, to show that Bud was "undesirable" because he "had not been turning in all the taxes he collected." One Marion Maddox claimed to have "substantial proof." An examination of city records showed that Maddox had paid $7.79 in taxes, when only $5.79 was due. "A simple mistake," Bud said, and paid the $2 from his own pocket. The rumor now spread as truth. Bud checked his receipt book at his office. The stub showed that Maddox actually had paid only $5.79, and Bud, inadvertently, had turned in an extra $2. It was the first time in his career that his honesty had been questioned, and he immediately challenged Maddox to produce a receipt showing any sum other than $5.79, which Maddox could not or refused to do so. Bud announced publicly: "Any man who says I collected more than I turned in is a liar." Maddox made a retraction in the *Chieftain*, and many Gilstrap supporters voted for Bud because they didn't approve of "dirty politics."[2]

In November the newspaper noted that, for the fiscal year, Bud had collected "over $9,270.00" for the city coffers.[3]

Nonetheless, Bud's enforcement policy was a lasting objection. He became disgusted with local petty politics, and looked toward possible reinstatement as a deputy in the federal service.

The term of Judge Thomas had expired in July 1901. Many letters and resolutions from chiefs of the Cherokee, Creek, and Seminole nations forwarded to Washington soliciting his reappointment failed to offset the powerful patronage wielded by Joseph G. "Uncle Joe" Cannon, influential member of the House of Representatives, from Illinois. Charles W. Raymond, a prominent attorney at Watseka, Illinois, and supporter of McKinley for his second term as president in 1900, was appointed Judge Thomas' successor. Judge Thomas opened a law office in Muskogee and was a recognized legal leader and upbuilder of the region until shot to death while seated in the warden's office at the state penitentiary in McAlester during a serious prison outbreak on January 19, 1914. Judge Raymond assumed his duties at Muskogee in August 1901, and became chief justice of the Indian Territory court of appeals.[4]

On September 6 McKinley was assassinated by Leon Czologsz, an anarchist, at Buffalo, New York. Vice President Theodore Roosevelt succeeded him to the presidency, and on December 7, Roosevelt reappointed Leo Bennett as U.S. marshal for the Northern District.

The morning of February 6, 1902, Ledbetter was preparing to depart for Muskogee to discuss reinstatement of his deputy's commission with Marshal Bennett, when news came that Sheriff

John Powers had been slain at Clarksville, Arkansas. Bud and Paden Tolbert left immediately on a gloomy journey to attend their old comrade's funeral and learn the details of his death.

At about 2:00 A.M. on the morning of February 5, the Bank of Clarksville had been entered and the vault and inner cash chest blown with nitroglycerine. Sheriff Powers, who roomed on the second floor of Mitchell & Son's drug store adjoining the bank on the east, heard the explosions. Partially dressed, he hurriedly descended the stairway leading into the alley to investigate. At the base of the stairs, he exchanged shots with a lookout stationed at the rear of the bank. As the man fled, Powers was fired upon from the front of the building. "Instead of taking refuge in the stairway . . . he returned the fire from the front, all the time advancing." Bullet marks on the building indicated that he had "forced the gunman back into the alcove or bank door . . . when he received his death wound. . . . The doctor could do nothing to save the life of the brave man and officer, and he breathed his last 30 minutes later. . . . A few that had heard the explosions and fight with pistols and gathered about the scene . . . hardly knew what to do or where to begin. The robbers had made their escape after securing about $1,200 in silver from the bank safe, leaving behind about $4,000 in gold and mutilated currency. . . . It appeared they had left town on a freight train."[5]

The entire country was searching for the perpetrators. Rewards totaling $8,550 had been offered by the State of Arkansas, citizens of Clarksville, Johnson County, Bank of Clarksville, and State Banker's Association, and "some of the best detectives in the country worked on the case."[6]

Bud and Tolbert were consoled by witnessing the tremendous throngs that attended the funeral. Powers had been sheriff for eleven years and could have held the office as long as he cared to ask for it. He was personally known by nearly every man, woman, and child in Johnson County, and all turned out with many from other counties and cities of the state and Indian Territory to pay him tribute. Further evidence of his popularity was shown by voluntary subscription of $1,500 to erect a monument to his memory—by far the largest tombstone in Oakland Cemetery.

Two months later, one of the robbers, John Derham, was apprehended in Wichita, Kansas. After Derham's capture, circumstances led to the arrest of his companion, Fred Underwood. Both were placed in the Arkansas state penitentiary at Little Rock for safe keeping. At the December 1902 term of the Johnson County circuit court, Derham and Underwood were tried and convicted for the murder of Sheriff Powers, and finally hanged in the Johnson County courtyard the morning of June 18, 1903.[7]

Back in Vinita, Bud still considered returning to federal service. But another attempt to oust him as city marshal failed in March 1902, and Congress again was tinkering with the Indian Territory judiciary.

By act of May 27, Congress divided the Northern District into two, creating a Western District. The Northern District now comprised the Cherokee and Quawpaw Agency, with headquarters at Vinita and other court towns being Miami, Sallisaw, Pryor Creek, Claremore, Nowata, and Bartlesville. The new Western District comprised the Creek and Seminole nations, with headquarters at Muskogee, and other court towns being Wagoner, Okmulgee, Sapulpa, Tulsa, Wewoka, and Eufaula.[8]

Judge Gill remained in the Northern District and established his residence at Vinita. Judge Raymond became judge of the Western District with Leo Bennett as marshal, yielding to the appointment as U.S. marshal for the Northern District of a Roosevelt "Rough Rider" friend, William H. Darrough.

Paden Tolbert asked for and received a transfer to the Western District. Marshal Bennett stationed him at Weleetka, in the southwestern Creek Nation, to work the Creek–Seminole border. He moved his wife Lucy and four children from Vinita to Weleetka in June 1902.

On August 26 Marshal Darrough transferred forty federal prisoners from Muskogee to Vinita. "They belong to the Northern District and will be kept in the Northern District jail for trial next week." The crimes "run from larceny to murder, and some of them are as tough as men get before they are hanged or die with their boots on."[9]

Despite Darrough's force of deputies and guards, the influx of friends of the prisoners and hundreds attending the trials as witnesses and spectators was an added burden on City Marshal Ledbetter. But Bud was up to the responsibility, hiring only one special policeman.

After the convening of the grand jury, Bud also cooperated in a "general crusade" being waged by the Anti-Saloon League against booze sellers throughout the Territory. "Superintendent Wooten of the league and league detectives spent some time in Vinita. Specimens of all concoctions sold and a mass of evidence was accumulated against the vendors of so-called 'mead' and other intoxicants." The work was "conducted quietly, but most thoroughly, and not only joint keepers but druggists who engage in the illegal traffic will be vigorously prosecuted."[10]

Interestingly, the grand jury found eight indictments against joint keepers, ignored one case, and a doctor who pleaded guilty to introducing and disposing of liquor was fined $1,000.

Bud served most of his second term as city marshal. On January 1, 1903, he was reappointed deputy under Marshal Bennett and stationed in the Western District, at Okmulgee.

Chapter 15

"... to his friends, as true as steel"

LITTLE IS KNOWN OF Ledbetter's stay at Okmulgee except in the recollections of long-time deputy marshal, A. R. "Al" Cottle.

Cottle had received a teaching certificate from the Normal School at Paoli, Kansas, in 1901. His ambition was to be a lawyer, and he took a teaching position at Holdenville, southeast of Wewoka, as a means of earning money to study law. Deputy Marshal Courtland Fleming, who was stationed at Wewoka, noticed the "efficient and cool manner" in which Cottle conducted his classes and disciplined his near-adult students, and the men became friends. Fleming wanted to transfer to Muskogee, which Marshal Bennett declined unless Fleming could find a suitable replacement. Fleming had "just the right man in mind"—Cottle's ability to handle the pranks of his students and his aspiration to be a lawyer "could meet the requirements" of a federal deputy. Fleming broached the idea that law work would aid in his studies, and Cottle agreed to take the job, "temporarily." Fleming got his transfer, and Cottle was sworn in on July 1, 1903. It was the custom to assign a recruit to a veteran deputy, and Marshal Bennett asked Ledbetter to "break in" the new lawman. Bud obviously performed his task well. Cottle completed his law course and was admitted to the bar, but never engaged in active practice; he wore a deputy's badge the next fifty years, serving under eight different marshals and during the administrations of eight United States Presidents—Theodore Roosevelt to Harry Truman.[1]

Cottle recalled that one of the highlights of his training under Ledbetter was "still-busting." Deep in the brush one afternoon he and Bud staked out a small clearing where three moonshiners were at work.

"This business was a bit more tense than a day in the classroom," Cottle said. Bud had ominously warned: "Never take any situation for granted—not even the commonplace raiding of a still."

He told Cottle: "You take the north side of the clearing, and I'll take the south side. When you see me step in the open, you come out, and we'll arrest the three of them."

Cottle quietly circled through the brush into position, hitched up his heavy gun belt, and watched intently. Boldly, Bud stepped from hiding and bellowed at the whiskey makers: "Raise your arms to the sky, you are under arrest!"

The men wheeled, recognized Bud, and offered no resistance. Cottle, remembering Bud's warning, leaped into the clearing, his six-shooter drawn. To his astonishment, the fierce looking moonshiners began laughing. Even Bud lustily "hawhawed."

Then Cottle noticed the source of their mirth. In his haste, he had ripped the holster from his gun belt and was resolutely pointing the holstered weapon at the lawbreakers![2]

Cottle soon settled into his deputy work at Wewoka, and by November, his tutor, Ledbetter, was Muskogee bound.

Marshal Bennett had reported to the Department of Justice the extent of crime in the Northern and Western districts during the six years he had been in office. He had "handled 5,823 indicted cases . . . larceny cases alone have been 2,084." There had been "356 cases of murder . . . forty-three cases now on the criminal docket awaiting disposition." Thirty-eight indicted murderers were still at large. Assault to kill cases, "which are almost identical, save the victims did not die," totaled 377. There were 200 prisoners in the Muskogee jail, "about all this time-worn structure will hold. A number have recently been released on small bonds to make room for those charged with more heinous crimes. The court docket is on par with the jail, as there are 720 cases either indicted or pending before the grand jury."[3]

Bennett needed a chief deputy to assist in "this growing volume of work," and he wrote Attorney General Philander C. Knox accordingly, on December 2:

> . . . There is within my acquaintance but one man who has the ability and tact and energy to do this work in a satisfactory manner, and that man is field deputy J. F. Ledbetter, with present headquarters at Okmulgee. This man has had years of experience as an officer . . . knows this entire district . . . knows the people . . . thoroughly understands the criminal class and knows where they range when scouting. . . . He is honest, straightforward and reliable, a man upon who I can depend with a certainty. . . . An incompetent man in this position would only add to my burdens and I would not be bothered with such a man under any circumstances.
>
> I therefore recommend and request that beginning January first I be allowed such additional deputy with headquarters at Muskogee; that his salary be fixed at $1,500 per annum . . . and that he be authorized his actual and necessary expenses while absent from headquarters engaged in the performance of official duties.
>
> Very respectfully,
>
> Leo. E. Bennett
> U.S. Marshal

It was the highest tribute anyone had paid Ledbetter. On January 6, 1904, he and Mary Josephine became residents of Muskogee.

Bud found the office staff, headed by Deputy Ernest Hubbard, deep in a mass of warrants, civil writs, and subpoenas. They welcomed Bud's assistance.

The regular term of court for the Western District convened at Muskogee on January 11, with 2,500 cases on docket— "2,000 probate, 200 bankruptcy and 300 criminal," nine of which were murder cases. It was estimated that, while the court was in session, the grand juries would return "another 500 indictments. The Muskogee court is the oldest court in Indian Territory, which accounts for the large amount of business and it is here that all the government cases involving the rights of the Five

Tribes are heard. . . . The jury venire shows sixteen grand jurors and thirty-six petit jurors."[4]

This was only the beginning of the spring circuit, which included court settings at Wagoner, Sapulpa, Eufaula, Okmulgee, and Wewoka, where separate dockets were taken up as soon as the Muskogee docket was completed. The number of cases in these towns equaled the number at Muskogee, for a total of 5,000 cases in the district. The juries changed at each court town; it cost the United States $500 per day to run the sessions; and it took until past mid-April to transact this largest volume of business for a single term in Western District court history.

Bud was just completing his three-month swing through the court towns when he lost his closest friend, Paden Tolbert.

Since being elected at Weleetka, Tolbert had been conducting business on the side—a common practice for deputy marshals. Morton Rutherford had entered civilian life as a lawyer and formed a partnership with fellow attorney Jesse Hill, contracting with the Fort Smith and Western railroad to locate townsites as its line progressed through the Creek Nation toward Oklahoma Territory. Because new towns were prone to lawlessness before stable citizens could set up workable governments, Rutherford and Hill had involved Tolbert in founding Okemah in 1902.

After disposing of their Okemah contract, the three partners surveyed a new townsite some fifteen miles further west on a partly timbered divide between the Deep and North forks of the Canadian. Tolbert's presence and his work on the sale of lots had brought about twenty families to the site immediately, and at the first town meeting, the site was named Tolbert in honor of its guardian hero. The post office department objected because of a difference of one letter in the name and that of Colbert, in the Chickasaw Nation. So the name Paden was selected. By the end of 1903, Paden, I.T., was a thriving town of several hundred citizens.

Tolbert suffered from oak poisoning and a lung ailment resulting from his years of exposure to the elements while riding Indian Territory. Early in January, he had resigned his deputy's commission and accepted a job with the Fort Smith and Western as claims agent and railroad detective. His condition worsened, and he had sought relief in the healing waters at Hot Springs, Arkansas, where he died of lung congestion on April 24, at age forty-three.

It was a sad day for Ledbetter and Captain White of Vinita, as they attended the last rites and interment at Clarksville. Bud and Captain White paid Tolbert tribute, saying he was "brave and fearless . . . to his friends, as true as steel." The citizens of Paden, I.T., especially grieved the loss of their hero, and by petition, had his wife appointed postmistress. Tolbert was the only deputy marshal in U.S. history to have a full-fledged town named for him.

Four days after Tolbert's death, Congress provided for an additional judge in each of the four Indian Territory districts to handle the increasing case load. They were not to be members of the court of appeals, however. Further, "all the laws of Arkansas heretofore put in force . . . are hereby continued and extended . . . so as to embrace all persons and estates in said territory, whether Indian, freedman, or otherwise, and full and complete jurisdiction is hereby conferred upon the district courts in the settlement of all estates of decedents, the guardianship of minors and incompetents, whether Indian, freedman, or otherwise." Thus, the Indian courts were divested of *all* jurisdiction; territorial courts would exercise full powers as courts of chancery and courts at law until statehood. William R. Lawrence, of Danville, Illinois, was appointed as the additional judge for the Northern District. Louis Sulzbacher of Missouri became the additional judge for the Western District before whom Marshal Bennett and his deputies could bring prisoners for arraignment and trial.[5]

Bud sought solace from the loss of Tolbert by winding up his duties with the spring term of courts. On April 30 he sent eighteen prisoners, in charge of Deputy Hubbard, to the federal jail at Fort Smith, where many Territory prisoners convicted of lesser offenses were still being housed to serve their time. On May 19 he took "personal charge" of a group of eight felons bound for Leavenworth. "After these shipments were made only 143 prisoners were left in the Muskogee jail," which Marshal Bennett reported as "the lowest figure reached at this institution in many years."[6]

Chapter 16

Suppressing the Blacks

T HE LEDBETTERS WERE PLEASED living in Muskogee—touted in 1904 as the "Queen City of the Arkansas River Valley." Mary Josephine readily entered its cultural life, attending women's club and other social functions, including concerts in old Gavagan Hall. Amusement lovers had become dependent on the hall's limited facilities since the destruction of the Turner Opera House in the Great Fire of 1899.

The city was permanent headquarters of the Dawes Commission and its several hundred employees; the United States clerk's office was a busy place with a large staff; the recording officers of the territory, the main office of the U.S. Indian inspectors, and the Union Agency of the Five Tribes added many more employees to the government payroll; more government-franked mail left the post office than from any other in the United States except Washington; and Gen. Pleasant Porter had his executive offices and home there. The streets and hotels were jammed daily with Indians, lawyers, real estate speculators, adventurers, confidence men, and grafters. Despite the efforts of local police, hop-ale and "uno" (you know) joints still supplied the thirsty. These shortcomings aside, Muskogee was, indeed, the most important commercial, financial, and industrial center in the Territory.

Everyone seemed happy and confident of the future—except a new problem had reared its ugly head and become a deep concern of the people throughout the Western District.

There were 5,000 former slaves sharing equally in tribal annuities and 800,000 acres of land worth a million dollars taken from the Cherokee and Creek Indians, who had opposed it in the treaties of 1866 and still opposed it. Blacks who were on plantations in the Creek Nation during the war had secured the best land—"an irritating subject to the Indian." These freedmen also could vote and hold office—privileges yet denied whites, except intermarried citizens. In fact, they dominated the House of Warriors of the Creek Council, and occupied a significant number of seats in the House of Kings. As a further blow to Creek pride, freedmen could sell their allotments at will, while those of the Indian were restricted and could be disposed of only after approval of the Department of the Interior. Many freedmen refused to sell any portion of their allotments and became prosperous farmers and businessmen, but others "disposed of their property in an orgy of land sales, often for less than its actual value, squandered the proceeds and were now indigents." This "superiority by law over white non-citizens and former owners and masters of Indian blood" had precipitated bitter clashes. "Many homes and businesses kept firearms within easy reach." A race war "seemed unavoidable."[1]

In April 1902 Will Haynes, a thirty-four-year-old white man, was found in a vacant lot in the business section of Wagoner, stabbed to death by a pair of scissors found lying near his body. "Robbery was thought to have been the motive for the revolting crime. . . . Six men and three women, all negroes, were arrested in connection with the murder, and owing to the threats of lynching at Wagoner," were brought to Muskogee for questioning and disposition.[2]

Secret clubs had been organized, allegedly to protect black rights. One of the first cropped up at Eufaula in the summer of 1902.

Tom "Witty" Hope, a freedman "about forty years of age, nearly six feet in height and powerful," had 160 acres of "as good land as can be found in the Creek Nation." He did little work on it and had rented to white settlers. His wife objected. He "forbid her to join the society, but she ignored his command." When she returned from a meeting the night of August 20, he "attacked her with a huge butcher knife, cutting her breast from collar bone to the waist." She ran about 100 yards from the house and fell on the ground. Hope then "grasped an ax . . . and with one blow to her neck, the head was severed from the trunk. . . . While the flesh was still quivering the fiend stepped in the blood that he had shed and exhalted in his diabolical work." A courier notified Grant Johnson, the black deputy marshal at Eufaula. Johnson hastened to the scene, but found Hope in no mood to escape, sitting on his porch. The deputy delivered his prisoner at Muskogee the following afternoon. At his arraignment in commissioners court, Hope said: "No, I don't want no lawyer. Dat paper [the *Phoenix*] tells all about de killing. Dat paper 'clares me," meaning it was his declaration and he didn't want the services of an attorney. Hope was bound over for action of the September grand jury.[3]

In November 1902 rebel freedmen occupied a site on the Ozark and Cherokee Central branch of railroad twenty-five miles west of Okmulgee, vowing to build a town "exclusively for negroes. Negroes will own the land and all the stores, gins, banks, mills and shops. They will have their own mayor, city council, and everything else. Lots are priced at $18."[4]

Matters intensified in 1903 at Braggs, a railroad town across the Arkansas, twelve miles southeast of Muskogee.

A white man named McBloom had furnished evidence that sent two blacks, Sam Roach, and Jim Taylor, to prison. The pair returned from the penitentiary in April, dropped off the train, and announced that there would be "hell in Braggs before long." The morning of May 5, Marshal Bennett's office was notified that "a riot had broken out, all communication lines had been cut, and it was feared the race trouble that had been brewing in the town for two years would have dire results." The youth who brought the message told how "McBloom stepped out his back door when he was fired upon by negroes who were concealed in his corn crib. McBloom dodged back into the house and grabbed his gun . . . called to the boy to run for help, that the negroes were murdering him. The boy heard a fusillade as he left." A ferryman on the Arkansas came in, stating he "could see women and children leaving the houses in the bottoms and gathering in one house . . . could also hear a lot of shooting." Shortly afterward, a black woman whipped her team into Muskogee, "shouting there was a negro uprising in which six white men were killed and others wounded." She was so wildly excited that Marshal Bennett "placed not much credence in her story," but dispatched Deputy Dave Adams and a posse to Braggs at once.[5]

Adams and his posse "found everything quiet [but] nearly everybody was carrying a pistol, Winchester or shotgun. One man had been wounded but it was impossible to find out who did it." The officers brought in seventeen whites and blacks, including Roach and Taylor. "All were charged with rioting. A few gave bond and were released. Adams does not look for any further trouble."[6]

On June 16 Paden Tolbert and a posse had raided a black camp on the Fort Smith and Western railroad near Paden. "A scheme to rob the pay car was apprehended and the marshal duly notified." The camp was surrounded at night "for the purpose of capturing all arms that might be secreted in the tents. . . . the negroes took alarm and began firing at the officers." A black man who went by the alias of the "Coosa Mountain Kid," wanted for murder in Alabama, "was hit in the left side with a shotgun . . . returned the fire fruitlessly . . . received another shot in the right side from the same gun, fell to the ground, and was making an effort to use his revolver, when a pistol shot quieted him. . . . Two negroes were wounded, six of the gang captured, and the officers also secured upward to thirty Winchesters and six-shooters."[7]

It had been Tolbert's last major action as a lawman before his death.

Ledbetter's first involvement in the racial problem came on May 26, 1904. He had just returned to Muskogee from delivering the eight federal prisoners to Fort Leavenworth.

At Sodam, a black settlement in the Arkansas bottoms ten miles west of Muskogee, a black man named Alex Vickering had raped a Mrs. C. M. Dunbar. The pursuit of Vickering by white men had precipitated trouble. The whites were arming, accusing the blacks of harboring the rapist, and the blacks were sending their families out of the settlement. James Vinhook, who lived in the vicinity, reported that "some unknown persons had appeared at his place, threw the furniture out of his home, and left notice for him to leave the country before nightfall or be killed." Vinhook believed they were whites who had accused him of assisting Vickering to escape.[8]

Bud hurried up the Arkansas. A black suspect drifting in a boat down the Illinois River had been arrested at Illinois Station and taken to Wagoner. Wagoner was under intense excitement, and a lynching was narrowly averted before the prisoner was proven not to be Vickering. Bud struck a fresh trail that night where Vickering had discarded the clothes he was wearing when he raped Mrs. Dunbar. Vickering had obtained new clothing and a good horse, and had armed himself. It was the last he was ever seen or heard of again. Bud stationed special officers at Sodam until things quieted down, but race feelings there simmered for some time.

At Wybark, ten miles north of Muskogee, "a white man was not allowed to stop after sunset and the negroes had everything their own way." On the eve of their Fourth of July celebration, whiskey peddlers distributed their wares and "the negroes got riotous. M.K.&T. trains passing through the town were stoned and many windows broken. An express messenger was injured by the flying missiles." Jim Patterson, the postmaster, took a gun away from John Brown, who was drunk. On Brown's promise of good behavior, Patterson "gave the gun back, but no sooner had Brown got the gun than he started a row with Patterson. The latter was shot and will likely die."[9]

The rioting stopped when local officers summoned Ledbetter with a squad of deputies from Muskogee.

The Fourth of July celebration at Wewoka was the scene of triple tragedy and almost a riot. "Excursions planned by the colored population, which largely predominates this section," were run from Okemah, Wetumka, and Holdenville, and "crowds of pleasure-hunting negroes filled the town to over-

*James Franklin "Bud"
Ledbetter—as deputy
U.S. marshal in the
Northern and Western
districts of Indian
Territory (1890s and
early 1900s).*

*James Franklin "Bud"
Ledbetter—as sheriff
of Muskogee County,
Oklahoma (1912–
1914).*

Above:
John Powers served with Ledbetter as deputy sheriff of Johnson County, Arkansas. They became known as the Johnson County "invincibles." John became sheriff of Johnson County, and was slain in an attempt to thwart a bank robbery at Clarksville, Arkansas, February 5, 1902.

Left:
Paden Tolbert, deputy sheriff, Johnson County, Arkansas; deputy U.S. marshal for the Northern and Western districts, Indian Territory; and Ledbetter's closest comrade. The only deputy marshal to have a town named in his honor. At his death, Ledbetter said of him: ". . . to his friends, as true as steel."

Above:
H. E. Ridenhour, former deputy U.S. marshal, Vinita's fire chief and finally chief of police, who acquainted Ledbetter with Vinita's history and political matters in Indian Territory.

Left:
Samuel Morton Rutherford —
U.S. marshal for the Northern District at Muskogee, who issued Ledbetter his first deputy marshal's commission in Indian Territory.

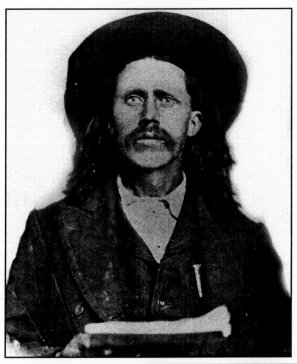

*Above:
Nathaniel "Texas Jack"
Reed, a Blackstone Switch
train robber in whom Led-
better's bullet put the fear
of God. He became an
evangelist.*

*Right:
James "Jim" Dyer, alleged
"brains" of the Blackstone
Switch train robbery. Convicted and sentenced to fifteen years in prison. His
case was finally reversed
by the U.S. Supreme Court.
At his new trial, he was
acquitted.*

Above:
William Frank Jones, deputy U.S. marshal who assisted Ledbetter in capturing the Turner gang.

Left:
Lon Lewis, deputy U.S. marshal who accompanied Ledbetter in his campaigns against the Green gang, the Jennings gang, and participated in the "Brush Court" expeditions.

Dave Adams, deputy U.S. Marshal who accompanied Ledbetter in capture of the Green gang, on liquor raids, and in the "Brush Court" expeditions.

Right:
William A. Lubbes, U.S. jail-er at Muskogee.

Al Jennings, whose gang Ledbetter and his posse routed in battle at the Spike S ranch and captured at Carr Creek. Paroled from prison, Jennings became a candidate for governor of Oklahoma, and later attempted to enlist Ledbetter for a stage performance with his movie, **Beating Back.**

Leo E. Bennett, physician, Indian agent, founder of Eufaula and Muskogee newspapers, and U.S. marshal for Northern and Western districts, at Muskogee, Indian Territory.

Judge John R. Thomas, first "supernumerary" judge for district courts in Indian Territory.

United States Court, Northern District, in session at Muskogee, 1897.

Above: United States Courthouse at Muskogee, Indian Territory.

Below: Creek Indians and freedmen receiving their allotments at the Indian land office in Muskogee, I.T., April 1, 1899.

Above:
Main and Broadway,
Muskogee — results of the
"Great Fire of 1899."

Left:
A. R. "Al" Cottle, long-
time deputy U.S. marshal,
who received his first
training under Ledbetter
in "still-busting."

*Deputy U.S. Marshal
Garey W. Teel*

*Samp Jennings, U.S.
Commissioner for the Western
District, at Sapulpa, I.T.*

Charles N. Haskell, railroad promoter in Indian Territory and first Governor of the State of Oklahoma.

Gen. Pleasant Porter, Chief of the Creek Nation, Indian Territory.

Right:
*Col. Clarence B. Douglas, editor
of the Muskogee Phoenix.*

Below:
The Al Jennings film, Beating Back, *portrayed deputy marshals as contemptible, blood-thirsty assassins or bungling cowards, and Ledbetter and his posse, in particular, as no match for the Jennings gang in the battle at the Spike S ranch.*

From the Saturday Evening Post to the Films

THE SATURDAY EVENING POST

An Illustrated Weekly
Founded A. D. 1728 by Benj. Franklin

SEPT. 6, 1913   5 cts. THE COPY

Al Jennings himself appearing in "Beating Back" the most famous of the Saturday Evening Post's "Human Document" series now produced in pictures. A bandit story you can show and advertise to respectable audiences.

Beating Back—By Al J. Jennings and Will Irwin

SIX REELS

"Beating Back"

By Al Jennings   With Al Jennings

(Produced at Thanhouser Studio)

How the most famous of modern bandits—a real Jean Valjean—pardoned by President Roosevelt—"Beat Back" at society until it recognized and honored him. Shows all of Al Jennings' thrilling life, including his hairbreadth escape from death at the hands of the law.

STATE RIGHTS GOING LIKE HOT CAKES

Remember, this rapid-fire story has been read by millions of Saturday Evening Post readers. **Bid for your state now,**

WRITE OR WIRE

Direct-From-Broadway Features

Room 1421, 71 W. 23rd St., New York

Watch for our Weekly Releases. Biggest stunts in the country.

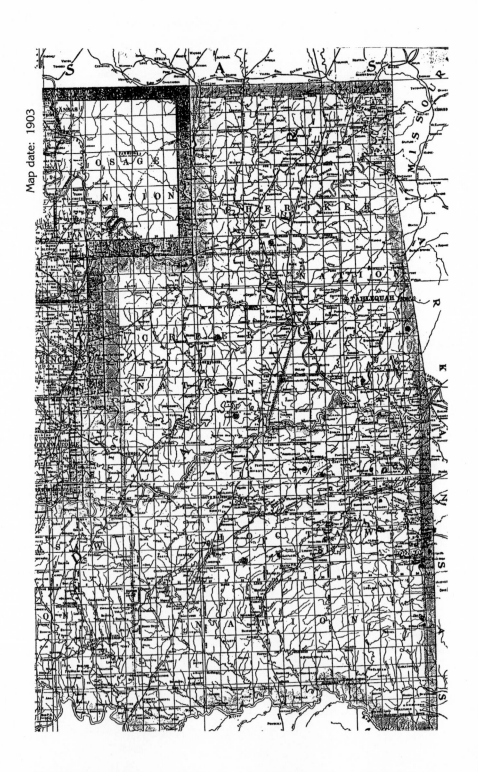

Map date: 1903

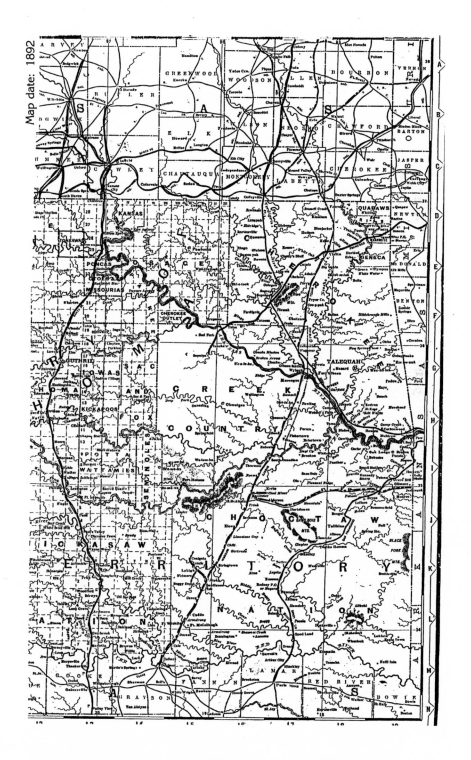

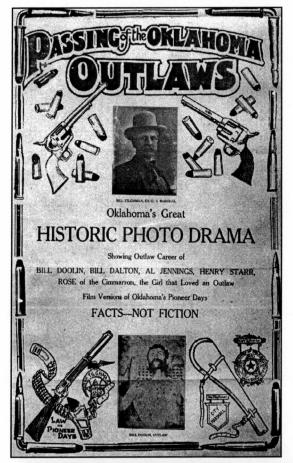

Passing of the Oklahoma Outlaws *produced by the Eagle Film Company to show the true sordidness of outlaw life in Oklahoma and Indian territories, and to refute the contemptible portrayal of federal officers in the Al Jennings movie,* Beating Back. *Ledbetter directed and played his own part in the segment depicting the battle at the Spike S ranch.*

1924 photograph shows Ledbetter and his raiding deputies with a mountain of confiscated whiskey stills — a typical result of Ledbetter's never-ending war on moonshiners during his last terms as sfcheriff of Muskogee County.

flowing." Liquor was in evidence, but "the crowd was orderly in the main until almost midnight," when Henry Stewart discovered his wife Mary in company with two other blacks, Henry Leonard and Jim Gaines. "A wordy battle followed," Stewart accusing his wife of being unfaithful and upbraiding the men in her company. "After some disturbance, Stewart drew an enormous Colt's gun . . . shot and instantly killed both men and his wife [and] made his escape before officers could arrest him. Great excitement reigned . . . a mob gathered and further trouble might easily have occurred but for Deputy Marshals Cottle and Cordell, who took the situation firmly in hand and quelled all incipient outbursts."[10]

Stewart fled across the South Canadian to Ada, Chickasaw Nation, where he was captured on July 7 by officers T. E. Brints and R. C. Crouch, and released to Wewoka deputies. "A pearl-handled .41 caliber six-shooter," taken from him by the Ada officers, "had two chambers loaded and the remainder discharged. It was these four shots that did the fatal work."[11]

Whiskey in Wewoka and other towns above the South Canadian was easily obtained from saloons and distilleries that were legal in Oklahoma Territory and thrived in the border or "line" places like Violet Springs, the Corner, Keokuk Falls, and Young's Crossing, which had been bypassed by the Fort Smith and Western railroad. Indians and freedmen had only to cross the border to drink, and the saloon towns readily supplied bootleggers in the Seminole and Creek nations.

Like Cottle at Wewoka, Deputy Marshal Ed Fink at Wetumka had his hands full. He had been in the service three years and was a tried officer. Less than a year previous he had been beaten and left for dead by blacks supplying whiskey at a society meeting, but had recovered and stuck to the dangerous business of a deputy. Monday night, November 28, word reached Muskogee that he had been slain near the Deep Fork of the Canadian.

There had been no racial outbreak at Wetumka. Fink had intercepted four Indians bringing whiskey from Keokuk Falls; they "had resisted arrest and killed him." Two of the Indians were in custody at Wetumka; the other two had escaped, "going toward the Creek–Seminole border."[12]

Marshal Bennett sent deputies to Wetumka and "notified every deputy on the west side of the Creek Nation." By morning, nearly seventy-five officers and possemen were scouring the country for the fugitives. Sam Miller and Boley Johnson, the Indians held at Wetumka, were brought to the Muskogee jail. "They denied taking part in firing on the marshal," stating that "Jim Tiger and Peter Fish, who had escaped, done the shooting."[13]

The posses found no trace of Tiger or Fish. Tiger had relatives at Eufaula, all full-blood Snake Indians, which caused Ledbetter to believe the pair had doubled back eastward to Eufaula or some hideout in the confluence of the Deep Fork and South Canadian. He entrained with horse and saddle for Eufaula, and picked up Deputy Grant Johnson.

The black deputy had brought dozens of bad men to the U.S. district and commissioners court since first commissioned at Fort Smith in 1893, re-commissioned in the Northern District in 1896, and retained by Marshal Bennett in 1897. Bud had worked with him occasionally and considered him an effective officer. Johnson knew the Tigers well. In 1899 he had wounded and captured John Tiger, after Tiger killed three men during a drunken spree at Eufaula, and had prevented his lynching by the aroused townspeople.

Bud and Deputy Johnson began a search of the trails toward Wetumka. On the evening of December 4 they intercepted Tiger and Fish ten miles southwest of Eufaula, near Melette, and took them without resistance. Tiger "confessed to the killing of Deputy Fink," but claimed "Fish fired the death shot."[14]

Fish was convicted at Muskogee in November 1905.[15] Deputy Fink's remains were taken to his native Chase County, Kansas, and interred in the cemetery at Elmdale.[16]

Bud's saddle had hardly cooled Saturday night, December 24, when he received a hurry-up call to come to Boynton, a trading center halfway between Muskogee and Okmulgee on the Frisco branch of the railroad. "City Marshal Warmick attempted to arrest a drunken negro, when he was set upon and badly beaten . . . also cut in the side and one hand badly gashed." A number of citizens had "rescued him from the hands of the blacks, but were unable to cope with the situation. . . . Fully 100 negroes prowled the town, cursing and threatening, heavily armed and stimulated by intoxicants."[17]

Bud summoned Deputies Hubbard and Al Cottle (Cottle had been transferred to Muskogee in November, less than a week before the murder of Deputy Fink). He telegraphed City Marshal Warmick that they would arrive on the first train. Cottle, reminiscing about the outbreak years later, said: "That wire saying Bud and his boys were on the way put the scare into those rioters . . . when we arrived at Boynton most all of them had sought shelter. We arrested one white and twenty-one blacks for being involved, without firing a shot."[18]

Chapter 17

Oil and Prohibition

THE FIRST COURT TERM FOR the Western District in 1905 opened at Muskogee on January 9, with an even larger number of criminal cases on docket than in January 1904—a total of 500, nine of them for murder. However, serving writs and protecting the court moved much faster for Ledbetter and the other deputies due to radical changes made in court procedure by Judge Raymond and an additional district judge, Louis Sulzbacher.

Heretofore somewhat lackadaisical, decorum and court courtesy was now "demanded." The presence of loafers and the morbidly curious in the courtroom was "discouraged." Cleanliness and order was "imperative" upon audiences. "Juries in the past who, the judges thought, were not fulfilling their duty had been summarily discharged and a new jury empaneled. . . . Empaneling new juries had greatly slowed business. . . . On account of this, every effort was made in securing juries of the best citizens of the country."[1]

These new court rules brought considerable criticism for the judges. But dockets were cleared on which cases had been pending for years—"127 indictments had been returned when the ten-day session adjourned."[2]

The court situation at Sapulpa was "really in need of correcting." Judge Sulzbacher found himself "buried beneath a multitude of cases, a large part of which had been continued from term to term without any certainty of ever coming to trial. . . . It was impossible to get witnesses in many cases and the whole machinery of justice at his command was cumbersome and uncertain." To remedy the difficulty, Judge Sulzbacher appointed a committee of three attorneys to go over the docket and strike such cases as could not be brought for adjudication. Thereafter, matters moved forward aggressively. The *Tulsa Democrat* opined, however, "This condition will continue so long as congress plays politics and refuses to grant statehood to allow us to regulate our own affairs."[3]

With the court term ended, the entire marshal's staff joined in celebrating April 1, the sixteenth anniversary of the coming of the first United States court to Muskogee. A committee was appointed to draft a constitution for a permanent association known as the "Pioneers," composed of men who had played prominent roles in the court's organization and had witnessed its opening.

Thomas B. Needles, the first U.S. marshal in Indian Territory and now a member of the Dawes Commission, gave an account of how the court was secured before the judiciary committee of Congress the winter of 1888-1889. Napoleon B. Maxey, who was among the first twenty lawyers admitted to practice before the first court on April 2, told of the arrival of the first court officials:

> The train pulled in at 10 o'clock in the morning and a band met the party at the depot. The town was then a little rambling country village, with a few houses grouped about the railway station. The court officials who stepped off the train were Hon. James M. Shackleford, judge; Hon. Z. T. Walrond, United States attorney; Hon. T. B. Needles, marshal; and Major William Nelson, clerk. They were fresh from Washington, D.C., and each wore a tall silk hat.
>
> We took them to a little rooming house near the depot, the best hotel we had then, and one of our party called Colonel Needles out into the hall and said, "Pardon me, Colonel, if I make a suggestion, but I would advise all of you to leave your plug hats in the house. If you wear them up town the cowboys are likely to take a shot at them."

We never saw any of those silk hats again, and Colonel
Needles to this day wears a soft hat well pulled down over his
ears. . . .[4]

The anniversary celebration culminated in "Roosevelt
Day." On April 5, prompted by his love for "my boys," as he
termed the Rough Riders, President Roosevelt stopped at
Muskogee on his presidential trip to the southwest. Marshal
Bennett was in charge of the ceremonies, assisted by old Troop
A, of the Indian Territory Volunteer Cavalry. The reception
committee, headed by Judge Thomas, included ex-Marshal
Rutherford, now mayor of Muskogee; Gen. Pleasant Porter; Col.
Clarence B. Douglas, editor of the *Phoenix;* and Charles N.
Haskell, railroad promoter and banker who had built the
Turner Opera House, an office building, rebuilt the city's street
railway system, and become a leading figure throughout the
Territory.

Roosevelt climbed from the rear of his train to a platform
erected at the Katy crossing in the center of Broadway. Judge
Thomas introduced the president to 15,000 people who came to
see him and hear his short address. He told his enthusiastic
audience to "look forward hopefully to the day when they would
have statehood and gave them some wholesome advice con-
cerning the duties of the citizen of a state."[5]

Ledbetter missed "Roosevelt Day." Early that morning, he
had been called to the old Three Bar ranch near Chase, eight
miles southwest of Muskogee, where a farmer hunting his horses
had discovered the body of a woman.

The farmer's dog, scratching in the entrance to an old wolf
den, had dug up "part of a female's attire. . . . The farmer informed neighbors of his find, and the body was uncovered." It
was "wrapped in a well worn piece of wagon or tent canvas and
bound with straps in three places"— around the neck, the center of the body, and the ankles—"in a good state of preserva-
tion, though apparently there for some time." The woman had
been buried in her night robe, a tortoise hair-pin still in her
long black hair. "She wore number six leather shoes, weighed
about 160, was about 5 feet 9 inches in height, and 25 or 30

years old. . . . A bruise on the left side of her head indicated she had been struck with some kind of instrument or weapon."[6]

The wolf den set on a broad prairie where cattle once ranged, and a short distance south of the Frisco railroad. Bud was unable to determine whether the body had been dumped from the train and carried to the scene or brought there in some kind of conveyance. Several who viewed the woman believed she was a former occupant of a well-known house in Muskogee. She was never identified, and the case was referred to afterwards as "Ledbetter's Wolf-Den Mystery."

Racial troubles in the Western District, though still prevalent, took a back seat to the surge of federal liquor and gambling violations. Oil had become a fascinating and profitable enterprise in Indian Territory. An oil and gas company had been incorporated in the Creek Nation as early as 1895. Oil discovered east of the railroad in Muskogee in 1896 and a small pool discovered in the southeast part of the city in 1903 had turned these areas into a forest of derricks. Discoveries at Red Fork between 1901 and 1904 had boomed Tulsa, and other oil towns were in the making as numerous companies sought rights to lease and drill on Indian lands. Big money coming in for development! More hotels and office buildings to accommodate promoters and traders! More stores to supply the increasing needs of the cities! And the attendant riffraff—bootleggers, gamblers, and grafters of all color, in all garbs and of every imaginable odor—preyed on this growth in wealth and activity.

Prohibitory laws relating to liquor, impressed in the Intercourse Act of 1834, which had created "Indian Territory," had been one of the most desired aspects of the government of the Five Tribes, since their removal west of the Mississippi. Tribal temperance societies now demanded that, if a new state be formed of the Twin Territories and admitted to the Union, Congress should include a provision prohibiting the manufacture and sale of intoxicants for twenty-one years and thereafter until the people of the state should amend the constitution.

The United Brethren in Christ, Indian Territory Church Federation, Woman's Christian Temperance Union, Church Federation for Prohibition Statehood, and other religious organizations in both territories were united behind the same goal:

expressly forbidden was the saloon with its adjuncts of vice, immorality, and crime. They claimed "assurances of a large number of senators and congressmen that their request would be granted," and that President Roosevelt had asserted "it is the only thing the United States can do in honor; the treaty pledges made with the Indians must be kept sacred and inviolate."[7]

These organizations vigorously pressured city and town authorities, and the U.S. marshal's office, commissioners and district judges in particular, to maintain the prohibition law already in force. Judge Sulzbacher was in apt agreement. As he told the grand jury empaneled at Sapulpa in December 1904 for the upcoming court term of January 1905, "intemperance is one of the most detestable vices cast upon the human family. Statistics establish the lamentable certainty that the origin of crime, in most cases, was caused by the turbulence of inebriation. . . . Such conditions are to some extent a defense, but, be this as it may, banish liquor, prevent its sale and introduction, and no such pleas need be made, and your criminal dockets will be reduced."[8]

This was also Ledbetter's school of thought—he had dealt with liquor so long as a peace officer. When Marshal Bennett ordered all deputies in the Western District to devote more attention to breaking up the liquor traffic, and appointed Bud to supervise a federal raiding squad, Bud welcomed it.

The demand for intoxicants was strong and more obvious in Indian Territory than in the States because of the difficulty of getting liquor from wholesale and retail dealers in bordering Arkansas, Missouri, Kansas, and Texas. Bud was thoroughly familiar with the ingenuity violators showed in finding ways to import their contraband. Often a consumer would board a train with a suitcase, go to some convenient border town, and return with it full of whiskey. Trunks, express packages, and even barrels containing whiskey were shipped by rail, and Bud would calmly wait for them to be claimed to make an arrest. Shoe boxes billed to a person who was not in the business of retailing shoes was a dead giveaway, and a parcel billed to an evidently fictitious name, though innocent looking enough, gave lie to its contents when weighed or gurgled when shaken.

Bud did err now and then. In August 1905 he observed two

kegs that were shipped into Muskogee and placed in the freight house to be claimed by their owner. He smashed the top of one—only to find black printer's ink. The *Times-Democrat* publicized the incident, stating: "The Sherlock of Uncle Sam's whiskey department . . . has lost his sense of smell."[9]

Bud acquitted himself admirably, however. He got word that a large amount of whiskey would be brought into Muskogee in two buggies from Keefeton, ten miles south, Saturday night, August 12. Accompanied by Deputy R. C. Fleming, chief of police Han Carter, and policeman Clark Compton, he set up a watch south of the city, where the contraband was to cross Coody Creek. "About midnight a buggy advanced, and two negroes, Joe Harris and Ernest Dodson, were arrested and held." Shortly afterwards, the second buggy and two black men crossed the creek. "Bud shouted, 'Halt!' but the pair did not heed the call, and whipping their horses, dashed away. . . . At least twelve shots were fired. One of the negroes, J. L. Samples, was hit in the left arm near the elbow." The four men were jailed at Muskogee, and Samples' wound dressed by the jail physician. "Fully 100 quarts of whiskey, stored in large gunny sacks, were found in the buggies, and confiscated."[10]

Later, Bud's zeal in pursuing bootleggers precipitated another incident which the *Times-Democrat* found amusing. Under the title "Bud Scores Another Great Victory As An Astute Detective and Booze Finder," the newspaper told how he stopped three Indians carrying pasteboard boxes.

"What have you fellows got in those lunch boxes?" Bud demanded.

"Only canned fruit," one startled Indian replied meekly.

"Canned fruit, eh?" Bud continued. "Never heard of it called canned fruit before. Peaches? Bartlett pears? Tomatoes and green corn? Did you get this stuff from a church member— sometimes they have it in hollow bibles and hymn books. Looks as though somebody might be working a new graft along the booze route, and I'll have to provide myself with a can opener. . . .

"You may go, but don't let that canned fruit go to fermenting."[11]

Chapter 18

Carry Nation
Presents a Hatchet

TULSA HAD BEEN A CONCERN of the marshal's office at Muskogee since June 1905. Incorporated in 1898 with a population of little more than 1,000, Tulsa had grown from a cowtown to an oil boom city of 7,200. The country just north and east lay in the corner of the Cherokee Nation, "not under the direction of the court that controlled the major portion of the city," but in the far southwestern reaches of the Northern District, "where many gambling houses did business and Uno men were reaping a harvest." Complaints to federal officials at Vinita had brought one deputy marshal; "the proprietor of one joint was arrested and the joint closed [but] nothing else has been done." Law and order groups had proposed changing the boundary line so as to include the few miles of the Cherokee Nation in the Western District, and thereby give the Muskogee marshal jurisdiction now under officers who had shown little interest in their plight.[1]

Tulsa's other problem lay in the annual change of its police force. Wess Kennedy, the first city marshal, had been succeeded in April 1899 by Charles W. Robertson, a popular early day blacksmith and wagon maker. Robertson was defeated in April 1900 by a strong supporter and enforcer of the law, Albert R. Baber, but in April 1901, Baber was defeated by Hiram A. "Hi" Thompson, a former deputy sheriff in Oklahoma Territory who

116

had moved to Tulsa in 1897. Thompson resigned in January 1902 to accept an appointment as deputy U.S. marshal, and later, detective for the Frisco railroad, protecting its trains out of St. Louis during the St. Louis World's Fair. L. E. Dean Hogan, appointed to serve Thompson's unexpired term, was defeated by Sherman G. Pender in the election of 1903. In 1904, as the oil boom expanded and Tulsa's population swelled, Ollie P. Marshall became city marshal and was given three policemen to assist him. In April 1905 Robertson was elected for a second term and given four policemen and a special officer named Lon Conway.[2]

This constant change in police personnel did not stabilize local law enforcement. Tulsa had become the hotbed of liquor sales, vice, and gambling in the Western District.

The *Tulsa Daily Democrat* described the city as "the home of some of the worst crooks, bootleggers and 'big-mitt' men the Southwest knows. . . . 'Sure-thing' games where unsuspecting men and boys are enticed by cappers to be robbed operate on the main streets . . . and officers have never turned a finger to stop them." Members of the police force interviewed by the *Democrat* stated "they had been instructed by their chief to let him handle the gambling here." Robertson countered repeatedly that "there was absolutely no gambling going on." Officer Conway "butted in"; assisted by policeman Abe Reneau, he made a raid that netted "cards, tables, two bushels of poker chips and a roulette wheel," which he "turned over to the mayor for safe keeping." Conway "was removed in less than twelve hours after he had taken action."[3]

Robertson became a more controversial figure by taking off his gun, uniform, and badge, going to the *Democrat* office, and assaulting editor William Stryker for printing articles alleging that he was not doing his job properly. Robertson then went to the police court, swore out a warrant for his own arrest, pleaded guilty, and paid a fine and costs.[4]

In mid-October Marshal Bennett sent Deputy Garey W. Teel to Tulsa. Marshal Darrough sent a deputy from the Northern District named McGlothin.

The evening of October 20, the deputies raided an establishment on West First Street and "arrested Roxey Green and

Walt Hughes on charges of introducing." Green and Hughes
were held in a front room on the first floor of the Gas Exchange
Hotel, handcuffed together, and placed under guard of policeman J. L. Atchison and assistant Tom Grider. Sapulpa was the
court town for the Tulsa area, and the plan was to take the prisoners there on an early morning train for arraignment before
the U.S. Commissioner Samp Jennings. "The night was chilly
and the fires were low, so Grider went for a bucket of coal.
Atchison went to the hotel office and "engaged in conversation
with the prisoners' attorney." When Grider returned, the prisoners had escaped. "The escape was reported at once to Deputy
Teel, who had all the bridges and outgoing trains watched and
notified officers at other towns." Green and Hughes were not
recaptured.[5]

The night of October 24 the disgusted Teel and McGlothin
raided the establishment of H. C. Francisco on West First Street
between Main and Boulder, arresting Francisco and four others
on charges of gambling. "The paraphernalia was taken out in
front of the building at 10 o'clock this morning and burned by
the officers. . . . A large crowd stood around the fire warming
themselves and looking as though they really enjoyed seeing two
poker tables, a bushel of chips, and five decks of cards go up in
flames." Each gambler was fined $10 and costs and told "the
next time the fine would be doubled."[6]

Said the *Democrat,* "The raid shows that federal authorities
do no want gambling to exist." But Tulsa citizens were hardly as-
suaged, and the newspaper asked, "What has become of the
gambling paraphernalia seized by Conway and Reneau some
time ago? Why not turn it over to the United States officers to
burn and save the city the trouble?"[7]

Nor did the existing conditions please Bud Ledbetter.

One of Bud's trusted possemen was Jake Elliott of Bristow.
Elliott was no gambler, but "knew the difference between a four-
card flush and an inside straight." He was not known in Tulsa,
and for several days "got into the various games." He made dia-
grams of each gambling and whiskey joint "so that, when the officers arrived to do their work, they would have no trouble closing every avenue of escape." Commissioner Jennings agreed to

help Bud lead the raids, with Deputy Hubbard second in command. Other members of the party consisted of Deputy Marshals E. N. Ellis and W. W. Freshour of Bristow; Grant Cowan of Okmulgee; and D. M. Webb of Weleetka, "to superintend the destruction of paraphernalia and bottle breaking."[8]

The raiders got off the train at Tulsa at 9:00 P.M. on Friday, November 3. Some "lookouts" spotted them and sped to William Thompson's gambling house on West First. Bud and his men sprang in pursuit and struck Thompson's place and a First Street joint operated by Tom Taylor, at the same time.

"Thompson sold no whiskey, and his business wasn't as good as his neighbor Taylor, but chips and cards, two crap tables, two poker tables and a number of chairs were seized." At Taylor's place "thirty-seven pints of whiskey were discovered in a leather suit case. . . . In a 'ratskeller' [German for cellar] reposed bottled in bond and 'rot-gut' moonshine and other favorite brands of the festive peddler. The bottles were smashed, one by one, on the railing of the back stairs." Taylor's gambling paraphernalia was "thrown out the back door into a vacant lot and burned." Thompson's paraphernalia was "broken up, piled in a heap and burned in front of the Alcorn Hotel, where an outraged people might see their position vindicated." Due to Jake Elliott's preliminary work, both raids were "absolute . . . not a guilty man got away."

Meanwhile, Bud and Commisioner Jennings descended on the Gas Exchange Hotel. "In one of the rear rooms, on which rent had been paid by two local sports known in the fraternity as 'Red' and 'Whitey,' they found and broke 51 pints of whiskey, about half of it being the ordinary peddler grade and the rest bonded stuff, pronounced extra fine by the attendant crowd of street corner connosieurs."

Bud and Jennings then proceeded to the Wells Fargo and Company express office, "where three boxes were bursted open and their contents, 226 pints of the bonded variety, were ruthlessly smashed and allowed to soak into the Frisco right-of-way."

The raids continued into Saturday morning, November 4. Sixty barrels of whiskey were found in the home of Paul Jones, a large quantity in the "chili restaurant" of Norm Sturgis, on Boston Avenue, and in other places.

The *Democrat* estimated that "500 to 1,000 gallons of whiskey" had been destroyed, and added: "Bud Ledbetter, the man who is terror to all wrong-doers, knows his business. He has a 'nose for booze' and can follow a scent as far as he can go in a day, getting results every time. The work of the Western District officers was eminently satisfactory."[9]

As congratulations were being showered on Bud on Saturday morning, City Marshal Robertson met him in front of the Bank of Commerce.

"You understand," said Robertson, "I didn't know there was gambling going on here."

Bud replied: "The hell you didn't—and you the city marshal? Well I be damned!"[10]

Later, Robinson told Commissioner Jennings that he was "just getting ready to raid the houses;" that, in fact, Friday night was the time scheduled for his raid. "Which of the two stories he tells is true?" asked the *Democrat*. "His position in the matter is pathetic. . . . Elected by the people because they believed he would conscientiously do his duty, condemned by the good citizens and supported by those who favor all that is bad, is a pretty serious and unfortunate situation."[11]

Policeman Abe Reneau was finally appointed to replace Robertson as city marshal.[12]

Commisioner Jennings bound the big gambling house operators and whiskey sellers over for trial in federal district court under bonds of $1,000 to $2,000. Those pleading guilty to lesser offenses gave this warning: "Gambling and peddling will stop in Tulsa if I have to personally raid the houses every day in the week. And the next time, it is going to mean jail sentences. There will be no fines."[13]

The *Democrat* of November 6 reported:

> There has been a general exodus of gamblers from town. . . . Peddlers have been inactive. . . . It is practically impossible to satisfy thirst, and the topers went back to their favorites—peruna, lemon extract, copal varnish, electric bitters and other territory drinks. Drug stores had numerous calls, but the visible supply of patents that drug but do not heal was soon exhausted.

The incident is now closed except that some of the bunch wonder if Bud Ledbetter et al. are likely to come this way again. The more philosophical say there is no danger, as "lightening never strikes twice in the same place." Others contend, however, that deputy marshals are like cyclones—no one can tell when they are coming nor where they will strike.

The raids were still the hot topic when temperance advocate Carry A. Nation, who thought herself ordained to wipe out Demon Rum, arrived in Tulsa on November 11. Mrs. Nation, not a large but a powerful woman, had made her initial forays in Kansas (a prohibition state) in 1900. For five years she had been rallying anti-alcohol forces throughout the country, leading attacks on saloons and other places selling intoxicants, and destroying rows of liquor bottles, furniture, and fixtures with her fiercely wielded hatchet. She had been arrested, imprisoned, fined, clubbed, and shot at for the activity she called "hatchetations," and was touring the Twin Territories in support of the demand to include a prohibition provision in the constitution of proposed Oklahoma.

Mrs. Nation spoke to packed assemblages in the opera house, the Tulsa Mothers at the M.E. church, South, and the revival services of the First Presbyterian church, stressing that she was "proud of Tulsa and the efforts made here on the part of some to clean up that devil—strong drink. Where you find saloons, you find bums, thugs, the idle and vicious. Take away saloons, and these classes will leave. No class of business ever prospers where saloons exist, except the saloon."

She told news reporters: "Bully for the *Democrat*. The *Democrat* is doing good work. Keep it up!"

She was dressed in black, with a Dunkard bonnet, and carried a small satchel over her shoulder containing a multitude of trinkets used in her work. In a grip containing her personal effects was a hatchet of the Kansas variety, with edge rough and having the appearance of hard usage.

"I'm glad I have no use for that in Tulsa," she said, "because Bud Ledbetter has beaten me to it. . . . To prove I'm not a law-breaker, I cite that Mr. Ledbetter did the same thing in Tulsa last week I did in Kansas, and they put me in jail twenty-five times."

Mrs. Nation set April 14 to 16 for a convention in Tulsa "to discuss the important subject of prohibition for the new State," and moved on for a fiery address at Muskogee. Spotting Ledbetter in the audience, she presented him with a special hatchet, saying, "I congratulate Bud Ledbetter, the Carry Nation of Indian Territory. Mr. Ledbetter, you are a peach!"[14]

Bud thanked Mrs. Nation for the hatchet. He did not particularly relish his new title, but he would carry it with him for years to come.

Chapter 19

"Anticipation" and "Realization"

DEPUTY GAREY TEEL REMAINED at Tulsa, miffed that he had not been included in the roundup of whiskey sellers and gamblers. Shortly after dark, November 17, he raided the Palace Hotel, "getting one peddler and thirty-seven gallons of whiskey. All but six bottles were smashed . . . the six bottles kept as evidence." His prisoner asked for a guard until he could be taken before Commissioner Jennings at Sapulpa, but Teel, "remembering what had happened the last time he tried to be merciful," placed him in the city jail. The next morning, Teel "went to the Wells Fargo express office and, squinting around, saw six suspicious jugs which were smashed and found to contain ordinary cheap grade whiskey . . . that Ledbetter and his posse missed in their recent raids."[1]

Apparently, Teel aspired to establish a reputation comparable to Ledbetter's. He did keep a lid on Tulsa, but soon was in trouble of his own making.

On December 6 he "arrested Sandy Thomas and Will Lacey and traveled all day looking for a United States commissioner." He found Jennings absent at Sapulpa. At Okmulgee, he "met with no better success." He reached Muskogee the afternoon of December 7, "found nothing doing," and lodged his prisoners in the federal jail. "Three towns, and not one commissioner," he complained to the *Phoenix.* "I wonder what the boys are doing anyway."[2]

This public criticism of U.S. commissioners didn't set well with Marshal Bennett, who considered Teel's mileage fees excessive. He thought Teel should have held his prisoners at Sapulpa until Commissioner Jennings returned.

Teel got in deeper water two weeks later. His wife had died some time before, leaving him with a small son and three daughters to raise. The eldest daughter had recently married and was living in Joplin, Missouri. The boy and two younger girls, "growing into sweet womanhood," resided at Sapulpa, where Teel provided them a house and a buggy for transportation. Shortly before Christmas, he went to Joplin and brought the married daughter to Sapulpa to be with her brother and sister over the holidays. Upon his return, he was informed by the older girl that Frank Vest, a local Lothario, had forced her to drive him in the buggy to Mounds, some twelve miles away. "Vest had whiskey and tried to make her drink with him, which she refused, and he was ungentlemanly in other ways. The boy, while searching for his sister, saw her coming home in the evening, and she was weeping." Teel promptly sought out Vest. "The young man wanted to apologize," but Teel "wanted no apology." He beat Vest over the head so severely with his revolver that the youth "was in the hands of a physician at the Sapulpa hospital, his condition very uncertain."[3]

Though Teel was "justly proud of his girls," Sapulpa citizens declared his action "outrageous." Fortunately, Vest recovered, and the deputy "tried to redeem himself" by seizing 400 bottles of whiskey that came into Tulsa by rail the night of January 10, 1906. "Seventy-five pints were addressed to Tulsa people . . . seventy-five were on their way to Bartlesville . . . the remaining 250 pints, which Deputy Teel calls 'nigger whiskey,' were billed to Haskell." Teel destroyed the entire 400 bottles "at his regular smashing post on the Frisco right-of-way." He declared Tulsa "a natural distributing point for a radius of 50 miles," and claimed to have "spilled more whiskey than any other deputy in the territory."[4]

Still, Sapulpa citizens pressed for his resignation, and the revelation that he was patronizing the very class he pursued became his undoing.

"He frequented gambling houses, in particular Tom Taylor's place, with a roulette wheel, crap game and poker playing going full blast in his presence. . . . A bottle was brought in and Mr. Teel and two other parties all took a drink." The night of January 30 he was "drunk in the gambling room over Brady's store," and on the streets afterwards, "conducted himself unbecoming an officer . . . abusing one good citizen by striking him over the head with a revolver and then placing him in jail." So said the affidavit sworn to before a notary public by a former policeman, Orrington "Red" Lucas, and there were "enough witnesses to prove his statement." Three other citizens were "preparing allegations of official misconduct" when the Lucas affidavit reached Marshal Bennett's office.[5]

Bennett announced the matter would be "probed to the bottom." The charges were forwarded to Attorney General William H. Moody in Washington, and "an inspector from the Department of Justice came to Tulsa and Sapulpa to look into the whole affair." Efforts were made to show that Marshal Bennett had "repeatedly been told of Teel's acts, but in every instance had whitewashed them." All of which was unproved and denied by Bennett.[6]

Deputy Teel was dismissed from the service.*

Ledbetter kept aloof of the controversy, undisturbed by Teel's claim of being the top whiskey raider in the Territory. Bud had other fish to fry.

William Melette, the new U.S. attorney for the Western District, issued orders to stop the sale of "uno," "sunshine," "beerline," and other light drinks being introduced along the Katy railroad. While these drinks allegedly were only one percent alcohol, the Indian Territory court of appeals had ruled that drinks did not necessarily have to be intoxicating to be prohibited and these beverages were clearly substitutes to circumvent

---

*Teel continued his law enforcement career as city marshal of Miami, I.T.; city detective, Joplin, Missouri, police department; and deputy sheriff Noble County, O.T.

the clause of the law prohibiting malt and fermented liquors. Though some defense lawyers argued that any mixture containing less than two percent alcohol was non-intoxicating, Melette "instructed Marshal Bennett to have all persons selling same arrested, and if they were released and continued to sell the beverages, to arrest them again."[7]

Saturday night, January 27, Ledbetter, Cottle, and R. C. Fleming raided a Muskogee joint operated by Mickey McFarland; seized three barrels of uno, "in all 226 quarts;" arrested McFarland and a black man named Gordon, who was acting as porter; and summoned twenty-seven occupants of the place as witnesses. The barrel labels, signed by the chemist and brewmaster for the Rochester Brewing Company of Kansas City, stated that uno contained 1.90 percent alcohol. District Attorney Melette declared it contraband. Ledbetter hauled it to the courthouse, where "all 226 quarts were smashed against the brick wall of the building. The crowd gathered around and watched the foam mount up and engulf the broken bits of bottles and eagerly sniffed the atmosphere."[8]

Several uno shipments passed through Muskogee billed to Eufaula. Whites, freedmen, and a number of prominent Creek citizens living in this trade and business center for a twenty-square-mile agricultural and cattle raising area were deeply interested in the education and welfare of their people, and complained about the town's gambling dives and drugstores which served as illegal bars. While they commended the work of Deputy Grant Johnson, he was in the field most of the time and inclined to view the situation as the responsibility of the city marshal and a nightwatchman. They considered Marshal Bennett a home boy—he had begun his medical and newspaper career there—and they expected action.

Bennett sent Ledbetter to Eufaula to "look around." Johnson was absent, so Bud proceeded to raid half a dozen drug stores, break some bottles, and arrest the operators. This disturbed Johnson to the extent that he boarded the afternoon train to Muskogee and demanded if Ledbetter thought he was lax in enforcing the liquor laws. Further, he "resented" Bud invading his "territory." Bud said he was only acting on orders. Marshal Bennett, who had taken much heat in the Teel investigation, was in no mood for Johnson's harangue. He told Johnson that no deputy could claim any section of the Western District as private domain, and sent him back to Eufaula. That night, Johnson took "revenge" by raiding four craps games and jailing twelve men."[9]

Bud disregarded the tactic, but it piqued Bennett.

President Roosevelt had just appointed Bennett to succeed himself as U.S. marshal; appointed Judge L. F. Parker, Jr., of Vinita, to succeed Judge Lawrence in the Northern District; and appointed Judge Lawrence to succeed Judge Raymond in the Western District.[10]

On February 3 Bennett took the oath of office in open court along with Court Clerk R. P. Harrison and three additional U.S. commissioners—L. L. Mosher of Wagoner; W. C. Butterworth of Sapulpa; and W. R. Hoyt of Muskogee. All office and field deputies of the Western District, except Grant Johnson, were together at Muskogee for the first time in four years.

Bennett took the occasion to make appointments and reappointments of federal positions under him, as follows:

At Muskogee headquarters—Ernest Hubbard, chief deputy; R. C. Fleming, civil deputy; Dave Adams, field deputy; Ernest R. Randle, Al Cottle, and Earl H. Coulter, office deputies; and Bud Ledbetter, special assistant to the U.S. marshal.

Division office and field deputies—George C. Gibson and Grant Cowan at Okmulgee; John H. Querry at Sapulpa; W. W. Freshour at Bristow; John L. Brown at Webbers Falls; Frank Jones at Checotah; D. M. Webb at Weleetka; James Garrett, black deputy at Boynton; Chester H. Fleming and John Cordell at Wewoka, succeeding H. J. Wooten (transferred to Tulsa to replace Garey Teel); and George W. Hanna, to succeed Grant Johnson at Eufaula.[11]

Johnson dropped out of the limelight and appeared but once more in the news, on October 3, 1909, when he was stabbed in the neck at Bond Switch (north of Eufaula) in an altercation with one Robert Watson.[12] He recovered from his wound and afterward did some service as a Eufaula policeman.

Said a Muskogee dispatch of February 22: "Ledbetter is now specially deputized to break up bootlegging in the western judicial district. . . . He has succeeded in driving out the negro and Indian bootleggers, to a certain extent, and is now engaged in the interesting process of eliminating the 'gentleman' boot-legger—the white men who bring in good liquor and dispose of it to a few of their friends they think is safe.

"Ledbetter is 53 years old . . . weighs 217 pounds and walks with a limp, the result of a broken leg received in an accident while chasing a criminal in Vinita while city marshal there three years ago.

"Bootleggers declare that he has a scent keener than a bird dog and can detect liquor in a box in a freight car as it runs past at twenty miles an hour."[13]

The *Times-Democrat* of February 27 added these humorous verses:

ANTICIPATION

I've got a little box acomin' on the Flyer
It ought to been here 'fore now,
I been waitin' an' waitin' for three whole days;
My mouth jest waters I'll vow.
It's a little brown jug of old corn booze,
The kind that brings good cheer,
An' make a man think he's a millionaire—
Dod Ding! I wish it was here.

REALIZATION

The Flyer came in with a rush and a roar,
And the booze man's heart was awful sore,
For down the walk a tall form bore
    with his hand on his gun and
    his hand on the door.
He seized that jug with ruthless hand,
That little brown jug of good old brand,
An' as it struck the ground with a dull, dull thud,
The booze man said, "God damn, it's Bud."

Bud stepped up his crusade. A shipment carrying a hard-ware store billing turned out to be thirty quarts of whiskey. One afternoon two trunks came in filled with wines and liquor. A bottle had been broken, and when the trunks were taken from the express car, Bud got a whiff of the goods. He followed the dray which detoured all over town before stopping at the home of one of Muskogee's most distinguished merchants. Bud confiscated the cargo and arrested the merchant. The night of March 16 he "landed the largest consignment of beer that had reached the territory in a long time, and broke up thirty-eight cases of quarts, while the thirsty citizens looked on in silent agony."[14]

Within a few weeks, Bud smashed so much jugged and bottled liquor and beer against the court building wall that the broken glass had to be hauled off in a wagon and the area reeked like the backyard of a brewery. Almost always the crowd volunteered assistance, but Bud declined all offers. And when he finished, it was jokingly said that he had to touch a match to the stream of whiskey running out from the wall to keep thirsty men away until the whiskey had soaked into the ground. The street urchins even honored him with a cops-and-robbers game named "Bud Ledbetter." The game "is usually played in an old warehouse where the boys collect all sorts of bottles and pretend to secret them. . . . One boy, who plays the part of the marshal, suddenly pounces upon the bottles, breaks them up and then the game is adjourned until a fresh supply of bottles can be secured."[15]

It seemed nothing short of murder interrupted Bud's raiding activities. The morning of March 29 he accompanied Assistant District Attorney Harlow A. Leekley six miles southeast of Muskogee to investigate the death of Lila Reese. Her body had been discovered by her husband, Felix Reese, in a thicket 200 yards from their house. "A bullet entering the back of her head and a stab from a knife in her neck told the tale of the foul crime."

The officers found a cigar box near the body, containing several personal letters, and "was known to contain $65 when taken from the house. . . . Tracks led directly from the house to the body and back to the house, the tracks of a man and woman." One set belonged to the victim; "the man's tracks fit the shoes of Felix Reese exactly." In the barn, Bud found a pistol, "which had been fired once, recently." Reese denied ownership of the weapon or knowing who had hidden it there. He was a full-blood Cherokee, twenty-five years old, his wife twenty-seven. They had been married for only two weeks. "Neighbors knew of no trouble between them, nor any reason why anyone should take the woman's life."

Bud let it go at that — temporarily. Digging deeper into the case the next day, he learned there was a credit of $2,000 to Mrs. Reese in a Muskogee bank; that she had sold her allotment for $2,500, and the $65 missing from the cigar box was part payment she recently received from the Indian agent for the tract of land sold." The dead woman's brother—contrary to what neighbors had told the officers—believed: "Reese murdered my sister to get her money." Assistant District Attorney Leekley obtained a commissioners warrant, and Bud "arrested Reese at the house as he was assisting in the burial preparations of his wife."

Though Bud was convinced he had his man, the commissioners court ruled the evidence "insufficient . . . purely circumstantial," and Reese was set free.[16]

As Bud put it, "You don't win 'em all."

Bud experienced another setback a couple of months later. On grounds that uno was "not an intoxicant," Mickey McFarland sued him and District Attorney Melette for the "cost price of the beverage destroyed by these officials" in the raid of January 27. Melette pleaded before Judge Lawrence that uno agents "admit and state that uno contains 1.90 percent alcohol . . . which means a quart and a half of alcohol in each barrel brought in"; that "when Judge Raymond was on the bench in this district, he held it against the law to introduce alcohol in any form or quantity," which was "in line with the decision of the supreme court of Arkansas, and the Arkansas statutes are in effect in this territory." Bud testified it was "impossible to tell whether uno contains one or four percent alcohol except by the way it makes those who drink it drunk." Judge Lawrence ruled in favor of the plaintiff, stating that, "The burden of proof lies on the government and this government has not shown that the beverage is intoxicating." He ordered Bud and Melette to pay $1 each, and McFarland conceded he "simply wanted to make a test case . . . did not want to make officials pay for what had been destroyed."[17]

The Tulsa and Muskogee press bemoaned: "Under this decision there will be scores of joints opened up for the sale of uno. . . ."[18]

Government officials promptly computed that "100 bottles of uno contain two quarts of pure alcohol. . . . By bringing in 100 barrels, two barrels of pure alcohol would be introduced or the equivalent of four barrels of whiskey."[19] On Friday, May 25, Melette issued this edict: "If anyone attempts to sell uno in this district, I will first secure evidence that patrons of the bar were intoxicated on the beverage and then proceed to cause their arrest and the confiscation of their goods."[20]

Chapter 20

Booze Oozes and a "Remarkable" Term of Court

THE LEDBETTER AND TEEL raids on Tulsa in November 1905 and January 1906 had done little more than stymie the city's gambling and bootlegging gentry. On November 22, 1905, oil was struck at a depth of 1,458 feet on the property of Ida Glenn, fifteen miles to the south, and boomed another shack and tent settlement called Glenpool, eventually to have more than 500 wells in operation. Rig builders, drillers, tank men, and others found Tulsa the immediate point for recreation, and Tulsa's whiskey business flourished more vigorously than ever.

In April 1906 Tulsa elected William J. Baber city marshal. Baber promptly announced his intention to "get a handle" on the city's vice and corruption. He conferred with Deputy U.S. Marshal Wooten, who quietly brought in Deputy Freshour of Bristow. The raiding squad included Baber's four policemen— "Michaels, Stokes, Kirk and Reynolds." Saturday night, June 16, "attacks were made on four resorts at the same time. . . . One posse went to the Robinson Hotel, one to Missou Simmons' place over Brady's store, one to Tom Taylor's place, and another to Charles Herwig's," north of the railroad tracks. "At each place gambling outfits were seized and taken to the city hall to await an order from the U.S. commissioner for burning them. Two negro joints also were raided and the paraphernalia destroyed." But, in some manner, the fact that there was to be a raid leaked, and "many places shut down before the officers reached them."[1]

Who provided advance notice of the raids was never known. Law and order groups blamed the federal officers and heaped criticism on Wooten and Freshour until Wooten resigned a few weeks later, again leaving Tulsa without a United States deputy.

There was no leak, however, in Ledbetter's plan to give the city a booze-busting it would long remember. This time, Bud joined forces with Special Agent for the Department of Indian Affairs William E. Johnson.

Johnson was forty-four, six-feet-two, 225 pounds, thick-chested, with dark, steady eyes and a stubby mustache. A native of New York, educated in Nebraska, he had served as a newspaper reporter, manager of the Nebraska Press Bureau, a feature and syndicate writer for eight years, and held executive editorial posts in New York and Chicago. He had veered into prohibition journalism as editor of a Funk and Wagnalls prohibition publication, and thence into detective work, when Congress appropriated $25,000 for a crusade against liquor traffic among the tribes in Indian Territory. On August 3 Commissioner of Indian Affairs Francis E. Leupp appointed him for the work, setting his salary at $2,500 a year, plus $3 a day subsistence and travel expense in the field. In the years to come, due to the frequency of night raids with chosen deputies and knowledge of what the press would print, he would be viewed as "ubiquitous" and ridiculed by the wet forces as "Pussyfoot" Johnson.[2]

Johnson left his family in New York and arrived at the Union Agency in Muskogee on August 18. Ledbetter found him agreeable in personality and fully capable for the duties demanded of him. It was the first raid for Johnson, and he readily accepted Bud's invitation.

The raiding squad, headed by Marshal Bennett, Ledbetter, and Johnson, included Assistant District Attorney Leekley; Muskogee deputies Hubbard, Adams, W. E. Coulter, and P. C. Williams; Freshour of Bristow, Cowan of Okmulgee, and James Garrett of Boynton; and Katy railroad detectives from Muskogee, Mel Bowman and Sam Harper.

The raiders struck numerous Tulsa joints on Saturday

morning, August 25, "seizing wine, beer and whiskey. . . . The scene in the alley south of the city building where most of the stuff was spilled baffles description. A heap of broken glass marks the spot. . . . The excitement among the peddlers and their thirsty patrons was intense, and a large crowd of morbidly curious followed the prisoners to the city building where they were brought before Commissioner Hyams. Six warrants were issued charging introducing and disposing of intoxicants. Assistant U.S. Attorney Leekley read the charges and one by one all pleaded not guilty." Hearings were continued until August 31, and bond fixed at $1,000 each. Two made bond, and four were taken to Muskogee. In the afternoon, following their departure, "Deputy Freshour went to the home of C.G. Sturgis in the southeast part of the city and got several cases of beer and two barrels of whiskey."[3]

This "booze-oozing attack" startled and angered a large number of citizens, who severely criticized it was a "grand stand play"; declared that "the worst places in the city were not even touched" because City Marshal Baber and his force had been excluded; and resented "the idea of a gang of federal officers coming from Muskogee to raid Tulsa, when Muskogee is much worse . . . not only for bootleggers, but for women of lewd character, gamblers and toughs of every description." The *Democrat* sided with City Marshal Baber: "Never a week passes that city police do not arrest United States prisoners and turn them over to the deputy marshals after the city feeds them four or five days. . . . The policemen get no fees for the arrests . . . the officers at Muskogee get the fees."[4]

Special Agent Johnson countered by calling attention to the Curtis Act of 1898: "It seems to have been generally overlooked here. Section 14 authorizes mayors of incorporated towns in Indian Territory to exercise the same jurisdiction as the United States commissioners and gives city marshals and police the same executive authority as deputy U.S. marshals in all whiskey cases. . . . This should give Tulsa a chance to do a little cleaning up on its own hereafter, without the necessity of waiting for Uncle Sam's men to act."[5]

Similar repercussions came shortly afterwards from Eufaula. Deputy Marshal Hanna, who had replaced Grant

Johnson, found vice and the flow of intoxicants thriving and asked for assistance. The morning of September 21 Ledbetter, Special Agent Johnson, and three possemen raided the town's drugstores and gambling establishments.

"Alexander Sellers, Henry Lambert and two other men named Mohert and Fuller are under arrest, Lambert for running a gambling house, the others for selling liquor." When officers attempted to search Sellers' drugstore, Sellers refused to open his 3,000-pound safe, and "Mrs. Sellers threatened them with a gun." Both were handcuffed under guard "while the officers broke open the safe with a 16-pound sledge. In the safe was found 80 bottles of whiskey."

Lambert was "just opening his gambling house for the day's business when followed in by officers who arrested him before a game had been played on the poker tables, or a roulette ball rolled. All the paraphernalia was burned.

"Under one drug store, a ten gallon keg of whiskey and another of alcohol were pulled from a partly water-filled hole in the wall by Bud Ledbetter. . . . The raid attracted hundreds of people, and negroes knelt and drank from the gutters the streams of liquid poured out by Deputy Marshal Ledbetter. . . .

"The entire town is in turmoil over the raid, which was as thorough as it was unexpected."[6]

Bud's raiding activities were interrupted Sunday morning, November 19, when Marshal Bennett dispatched him to "the all-black town of Taft," eight miles west of Muskogee, to investigate a brawl in which Ira C. Campbell, a well-to-do farmer, had killed George Sullivan, Sullivan's son-in-law Marion Warren, and a black preacher named Thomas Fields, who was a bystander. As usual, whiskey was a major factor.

"The crime grew out of the forced marriage of Sullivan's daughter to Charlie Campbell [Ira's nephew], who was a prisoner in the Muskogee jail." On Saturday Sullivan and Marion Warren (Sullivan's other son-in-law), met Charlie's father and Ira Campbell "to talk the matter over. . . . While drinking, the men became 'whiskey mad,' and the shooting began," resulting in the triple murder. Fields, hit in the arm and body by one blast from Campbell's shotgun, died Sunday morning.

Bud captured Campbell at Taft and jailed him Sunday night at Muskogee. "Campbell states that he shot in self-defense. . . . He will be arraigned before Commissioner Hoyt, tomorrow. . . .

"A peculiar feature of the case: — Two Muskogee business men had an engagement to hunt quail with Sullivan and Warren on Sunday morning. While on the train to Taft, they met Deputy Ledbetter, who informed them of the tragedy. They caught the next train to Muskogee."[7]

The Campbell case was added to seventeen other murders committed in the Western District since the beginning of 1906, most of them whiskey-related, and for which the alleged offenders awaited trial in the federal jail. From the point of "dispatching criminal business," the December term of court held by Judge Sulzbacher at Wagoner was the "most remarkable" in the history of the Territory. "The grand jury was in session four days and returned 139 indictments. . . . Sentences were imposed on sixty of the defendants. Thirty-one were sent to the Fort Smith prison, eleven to the penitentiary at Leavenworth, three to reform schools, and others to jail at Muskogee. . . . Fifty-three cases were continued, the defendants being in jail or on bond, and bench warrants were issued for thirty more who are at large."[8]

The Wagoner court ended, Bud further enhanced his "Carry Nation" reputation.

About mid-afternoon January 16, 1907, he strolled into Arch Wright's bar and gambling house in Muskogee, accompanied by Hubbard and Grant Cowan. "The place was crowded . . . the games were in full blast," and some time passed before anyone became aware of the officers' presence. "The crowd did not make the usual rush for the exits, but quietly submitted to arrest and were marched in groups of ten along the street past jeering throngs to the federal jail. . . . Forty-two gamblers who gave required bond of $200 or $500 were released. . . . The expensive gambling paraphernalia—crap, klondike, poker and senate tables, and numerous chairs—was broken up and burned by Deputy Ledbetter. A big bag of silver on the tables was confiscated."[9]

Keefton, south of Muskogee, had the reputation of being the "toughest" town in the Western District. Oil men boasted that the average camp they frequented "didn't touch Keefton for bad men and women, and the women were getting bolder than the men." Saturday night, March 2, Bud hit Keefton with a six-man posse in what one citizen called "a raid right," which "came as a surprise, although the better element had been expecting it." The officers "went through houses, searched restaurants, hotels and billiard halls. . . . No arrests were made, but numerous gallons of whiskey were confiscated and destroyed."[10]

Bud kept a running account of liquor he had seized and spilled since coming to the Muskogee headquarters in 1904. He included such forbidden intoxicants as Uno, New State, Waukesha, Mistletoe, Tin Top, Longhorn, Shorthorn, Pablo, Reveille and Hiawatha, and on January 19 reported "a total of 10,000 gallons, valued at nearly $80,000."[11]

The Keefton raid added significantly to his tally — a record unmatched by any single officer in Indian Territory.

Chapter 21

"A Little Fretted"

Shortly after noon, May 21, 1907, Muskogee was shaken by a terrific explosion. The twenty-two-foot flywheel of the Gas and Power Company—the largest such wheel in the Territory—flew to pieces. One five-foot length crashed through the east wall of the brick building, "passed over the street and three houses, and imbedded itself in the soft earth a block and a half away." A second portion "went straight up and lodged in the roof." Another tore through the west roof into the telegraph wires of the Katy railroad, suspending its operation, and "lit on Second street, narrowly missing a man who was driving with his daughter." Street cars were halted, elevators stopped between floors and fans were put out of commission. The board fence on the east side of the plant was shattered by bricks and mortar "blown from the wall by the force of flying iron"; the room in which the big wheel was located "looked as if it had been visited by a cyclone"; and "nothing was doing for two hours" until the power company restored service with auxiliary machinery.[1]

The commotion caused by the explosion hardly compared however, to the excitement of Bud Ledbetter's performance in the north part of the city five days later. The circumstances of this bloody tragedy had originated in 1905 and intensified as the African-American problem in the Creek Nation, like malt beverages, continued to ferment.

The constitution authorized by Congress for the proposed state of Oklahoma was soon to be submitted to the people of the Twin Territories for ratification. J. Coody Johnson, president of the Negro Protective League, saw the importance of having black voters fully advised as to its contents and, in mid-March 1907, declared "there had probably been no event in the history of the Negroes of said territories when more conservative action and sober thought is demanded." In notices sent from his Wewoka headquarters, he "urgently and earnestly" requested the selection of delegates "to convene at extraordinary session" in Oklahoma City on April 20.[2]

Johnson's plea for conservative action fell on deaf ears at Beggs, ten miles northwest of Okmulgee. The night of March 25 a "race war" erupted in which Scott Carolina, the instigator, was shot through the body and taken to Okmulgee, where he died soon after arrival. "He had been dead only a short time when the train reached Okmulgee bringing Mattie Rogers, a negro woman who was intoxicated. She proceeded to the house where the corpse lay and forced the people to vacate. The city marshal was called and arrested the disturber."[3]

A unique situation prevailed at Muskogee. An unusually large number of freedmen had come there to live and spend money derived from the sale and lease of allotments. Many took advantage of their new financial prominence and established businesses. The medical, legal, and other professions were well represented. The problem was not of their making.

In 1905 a black preacher at Wagoner named William Wright had organized a society of 200 members called the "Tenth Cavalry." Wright called himself "General Grant" in the circulars he distributed, and claimed to be an agent of the president of the United States. President Roosevelt sent the Secret Service to investigate, and the Tenth Calvary disbanded.

Some time later, Wright appeared at Muskogee in a new venture called the "United Socialist Club." Each member wore a badge of authority issued by a private detective agency in Cincinnati, Ohio, and was promised 160 acres of land to be deeded as soon as authorization was received from Washington, which could be expected shortly. Wright not only taught the Scriptures, but anarchy and the supernatural. He told his followers that, by wearing a "Voodoo" sack, they would be immune from death, and were entitled to occupy any property they chose without paying a cent.

A man named Trumbo owned a house in the south part of the city, occupied by a Wright follower, Lucy Curtis. Unable to collect his rent or get her to vacate, he moved the house to North Fifteenth Street. Unperturbed, Lucy Curtis remained on board, building a fire and cooking her meals while the house was en route to its new location.

There was other such arrogance and impudence as the club members grew bolder.

Carrie Foreman, another black woman, took over a house on Fon Du Lac Street, which its owners sold to a Mr. Sitz. When Sitz tried to collect his rent, he was informed of her Socialist club membership, authorizing her to occupy the property without rent as long as she wished. Sitz secured a writ of ejectment, which Constable John Cofield went to the house to serve at about 2:00 on the afternoon of March 26, and was seized by two black men armed with rifle and revolver. Cofield tried to break away and was shot in the chest above the heart. Guy Fisher, a white clerk for the Muskogee Wholesale Grocery Company, happened to be passing and was shot in the shoulder as he fled back toward town to give the alarm.

The two gunmen fled up Fon Du Lac to a two-story house at the corner of Fon Du Lac and Fourth Street, the headquarters of William Wright and his Socialist fanatics. Ed Jefferson, a prominent black citizen, witnessed the shooting, recognized the pair as Sam and Elbert Barker, and telephoned the chief of police, Charles Kimsey. Kimsey dispatched five policemen to the scene, then jumped into his buggy, drawn by a spirited sorrel horse, sped down the street to the federal courthouse, and relayed the information to Ledbetter.

Bud usually supplemented his .45 Colt's revolver with his .45 Winchester saddle gun, which fired black powder ammunition with a low velocity, leaden bullet. Kimsey's caller had warned that the Bakers might be wearing some kind of protective armor, so Bud snatched up a government-issue .32 rifle loaded with high velocity, steel-jacketed cartridges. He jumped into the buggy beside Kimsey. Deputies Hubbard and Paul Williams, who were on the courthouse steps, also galvanized into action and arrived on the scene close behind Kimsey and Ledbetter. Within moments, they were joined by Kimsey's policemen.

The Barkers stood on the porch, Sam armed with a shotgun and Elbert with a revolver. Two other blacks, Tom Jackson and J. T. Terrill, were positioned to the left and right sides of the house with Winchesters. Bud moved into the center of the street, the other officers fanned out behind him, and called to the four men:

"Throw down your guns and surrender!"

Sam Barker waved a Socialist paper which he said gave him the right to defy the authorities. Bud started to advance.

"Give it to Ledbetter!" screamed a woman in the house.

Sam Barker cocked his shotgun, but Bud was too fast for him.

The battle was on.

Sam Barker flinched each time Ledbetter's bullets struck him in the abdomen, and finally slumped down. Elbert Barker opened fire with his revolver. Bud shot him in the head, killing him instantly.

At the same moment, a black man named James Brown shoved a rifle out a porch window aimed at Bud. Black policeman Paul Smith caught the movement and fired, shattering Brown's right arm. A black named Scott leaned too far out an upstairs window, cocking a shotgun, and Bud shot him in the lower bowels. The man dragged himself downstairs, out the back door, and crawled under a wagon, where he died.

Jackson was shot through the neck and Terrill in the groin. Terrill escaped and hid under the floor of an old cabin near a brickyard in the south part of town, where he was apprehended the next day. William Wright and three other Socialists—Milo Wilson, Richard Gootch, and Allen Andrews—surrendered without a fight, and were escorted to jail by black policeman Frank Reed. Jackson and Brown were taken to the hospital, where Jackson's neck wound was treated and Brown's arm amputated.

When the shooting began, Chief Kimsey's horse had

dashed away with the buggy, but Kimsey quickly regained control of the vehicle. He and Bud headed for the jail to assist policeman Reed for fear the gathering crowd might try to lynch the prisoners. On Court Street, they met a mob of townsmen on foot, horseback, and in wagons, armed with everything that would shoot.

"Where's the riot? How many are dead?" they asked, breathlessly. "We're with you boys. . . ."

Bud checked the several bullet holes in his trousers, and drawled: "There ain't no riot. They're all dead." Then, ever thoughtful, he added: "You fellows better get hold of Charley Moore [the undertaker] and help pick up them remains."

More than fifty shots had been fired during the fight, and not an officer injured. Bud credited policeman Smith with saving his life.[4]

The Socialist belligerents had centered their fire on Ledbetter, and people marveled at how he had escaped. "I disappeared," he said. And that was the only statement he would make until editor Douglas of the *Phoenix* insisted that Bud come to his office for an interview.

"It's a whale of a story," Douglas explained, "and I want to get the details first hand—not only for my own paper, but for the metropolitan press north and east."

"Ain't no details, " Bud said. "I went up there to see what was going on. Them fellows started shootin' at me, so I killed 'em."

"How come they didn't hit you?" Douglas asked. "There were at least five of them. They probably averaged four shots each—twenty in all."

"Well, whenever I shoot I always take a step or two sideways, then I'm not where I was, you see."

"So you just stepped from one side to the other. Well, tell me, Bud, weren't you scared?"

"No."

"Were you excited?"

"No."

"Were you nervous?"

"I ain't never nervous."

"Well, you must have had some unusual sensation standing there with them men shooting holes in your britches."

"I don't know about sensation and such," Bud said. Then, as an afterthought: "I was a little fretted."

"Fretted? I'll be damned!" exclaimed Douglas. "Tell me, Bud —what fretted you? Maybe I can do something to keep it from happening again."

"Well, when I began firing at that porch fellow with that fancy little government rifle, I knowed I was hitting him in the belly every shot, and when he wouldn't fall it fretted me." Bud rose to go. "Tell you somethin', Colonel—never go after a shooting man with one of them new fangled .32s. Get you hurt if you do. Always take a .45—that knocks 'em down and they don't get up and bother you no more."

With that parting advice, Bud left, still the coolest and least excited man in Muskogee.[5]

In concluding his report, editor Douglas wrote:

"Investigation later, by Undertaker Moore, showed that Bud had been correct. . . . The deceased [Sam Barker] had a ring of bullet holes in his abdomen clear through him. Any one of these would have eventually been fatal, but they produced little shock at the time of impact, and zipped through the body without knocking the man down."[6]

Nearly every white man in Muskogee went armed that night, but "the negroes were not as dangerous as first feared, due to their dislike for the United Socialist gang. . . ." Territorial newspapers "colored" the affair and "played it up under bold headlines as a race riot," which was properly denounced by leaders of black community meeting at Jones Hall, and by a great majority of other citizens interested in protecting the name of the city. "The question of color never entered the tragedy," they declared. "Had the members of any race—white, black, red or brown—shot down an officer in this city in the discharge of his duty and attempted to kill other officials called to the scene, the results would have been the same."[7]

Socialist leader Wright denied any responsibility for the tragedy or knowing why the Barkers took refuge in the house where he lived. He claimed the "real head" of the United Socialists was "a very old white man with white flowing beard and tottering steps, without a drop of negro blood in his veins"; that, under the old man's direction, he had commenced operations of the Tenth Cavalry at Wagoner and come to Muskogee as his "superintendent." The mysterious white man was never found or identified. After "sweating" Wright, officers concluded that he was "crafty, crooked and insane."[8]

Interest in the Socialist club waned, and Wright left the Territory.

Chapter 22

10,455 Prisoners

LEDBETTER WAS BACK TO manhunting the summer of 1907.

The settlements of Starvilla, Porum, and Briartown sat in a triangle above the South Canadian, some thirty miles southeast of Muskogee. On July 4 area residents gathered on Dirty Creek near Porum for a celebration and picnic. Two wealthy brothers, Ben and Eugene Titsworth, set up a drink stand and hired a rover named Jack Baldridge to help conduct their business. Baldridge was known at Porum as a "bad man," who had led a "checkered career" using the alias Bill Williams. Deputy Marshal E. J. Sapper of Porum, and Sam Roberts, an Interior Department deputy under Special Agent Johnson, were on the grounds to prevent the sale of intoxicants to Indians. The officers approached the drink stand to destroy a keg of cider. Ben Titsworth objected, and while he was struggling with Deputy Sapper, "Baldridge drew a revolver and shot Roberts in the head," killing him instantly. "As Roberts fell, Baldridge lowered his gun to the head of Deputy Sapper and fired," wounding him seriously. "Calmly blowing the smoke from the barrel of his pistol, Baldridge slowly turned and walked away" into the timber along Dirty Creek.[1]

Four deputies arriving on the train from Muskogee were met by Porum's city marshal, "armed to the teeth and with the

Titsworth brothers in custody. . . . The boys had come into town and surrendered . . . confident that they would be able to establish their innocence." The deputies spent two days searching the Dirty Creek bottoms for Baldridge and "ascertaining his fighting record. . . . A bloody battle is looked for at any time, and the fact that the murderer is a dead shot, leads one to believe he will kill some of the officers, unless they catch him napping, which is not likely." Unable to pick up a trail, the deputies returned to Muskogee with the Titsworth brothers as prisoners, and "for the purpose, it is said, of getting more explicit orders from their chief [Marshal Bennett]."[2]

Emboldened by the officers' departure and his bad man reputation, Baldridge took the "extraordinary course" of defying the Muskogee authorities. His missive, received at Porum, read as follows:

> Here I am by the Midland Valley railroad bridge, sitting in the brush. I am not hiding and am not going to run away. At present I am playing solitaire and smoking cigarettes to idle my time. You can come and get me — it's a very short distance [half a mile from Porum]. But I will not be responsible for the outcome. Roberts was the eighth man I have killed, but shall probably have to finish a few more.[3]

Ledbetter told Marshal Bennett, "I think I can bring in Baldridge." He entrained with horse and saddle for Porum the morning of July 10.

Bud found the fugitive's campsite near the Midland Valley bridge, numerous cigarette butts, some left-over food, and horse tracks leading south past Briartown. He followed the trail all afternoon, losing it at times, picking it up again. At nightfall he discovered where his quarry had crossed the South Canadian into the Choctaw Nation. At daybreak, July 11, he came upon Baldridge on a lonely road in the river bottom near Whitefield. "The appearance of the marshal was such a complete surprise the fugitive had no chance to show fight."[4]

Bud took his prisoner, "heavily ironed," six miles west to Stigler and boarded the Midland Valley train. "News of the capture spread like wildfire, and as the train stopped at stations on the way to Muskogee, the platforms were crowded with curious people. A slender girl on the platform at Briartown cried out, 'There is the man who killed my father,' and broke down in tears. She was the daughter of the dead Roberts." That evening, Bud lodged Baldridge in the federal jail.[5]

At his trial, Baldridge swore that the Titsworths had agreed to pay him $300 to kill Roberts and Sapper, which the brothers denied. The brothers testified against Baldridge, eyewitnesses supported their claim that Baldridge had acted alone, and the charges of complicity against them were dismissed. Baldridge paid for his crimes, realizing the fallacy of defying the minions of the law whose six-shooters and Winchesters were called into play against hardened criminals almost daily — especially where the hunter was one of the Territory's most cunning sleuths, Bud Ledbetter.

Clashes over the statehood question between Democrat and Republican forces and party wings were rife during the summer. Characteristically, Bud remained aloof of the controversies, except once at Muskogee when he was sent to restore order.

The Enabling Act of June 16, 1906, had provided for fifty-five delegates from Oklahoma Territory, fifty-five from Indian Territory, and two from the Osage Nation to meet at Guthrie; that after their organization, the governor of Oklahoma Territory and the senior judge of the United States courts in Indian Territory should declare in behalf of the people that the delegates adopt the Constitution of the United States; whereupon the convention should form a constitution and government for the proposed state. Accordingly, on August 22, Governor Frank Frantz of Oklahoma Territory and Judge Clayton of Indian Territory issued a joint proclamation fixing Tuesday, November 6, as the date for the election of delegates. The proclamation was published in all newspapers of the two territories, together with maps of the various election districts. Realizing that their strength lay at the local level, political organizations cast about for likely Democrats, twelve Republicans, and one Independent assembled at Guthrie and organized for business.

As a matter of courtesy, the convention's powerful committee on counties deferred to the wishes of the delegate representing a particular district in fixing county boundaries, naming the county, and designating the temporary county seat. During a recess of the convention in March 1907, the Democratic Party State Committee met at Tulsa, agreed to hold primary elections for selecting their candidates for state and county officers, and called for territorial-wide primaries to be held on June 8. In these primaries, Charles N. Haskell of Muskogee defeated Lee Cruce of Ardmore, for the Democratic gubernatorial nomination. A committee of Republicans of national influence, who predicted that President Roosevelt would disapprove the constitution as framed and refuse to issue the proclamation of statehood, went to Washington and returned with a list of features the president considered objectionable. The convention again convened at Guthrie on July 10, and through the influence of its more conservative members, made changes to meet the standards of President Roosevelt. Thereupon, the constitution was adopted in its entirety, and the convention adjourned permanently on July 16.

Meanwhile, the Republicans chose the convention rather than primary method for selecting their state, county, and congressional officers. Muskogee Republicans met the afternoon of July 18 to select thirty-nine delegates and as many alternates to the state Republican convention to be held on August 1 at Tulsa, and twenty-nine delegates and as many alternates to the Republican congressional convention to be held in Tahlequah after adjournment of the state convention. The Tulsa delegates stood for a state ticket, Frank Frantz for governor, and for the constitution "under protest." Opposition to the constitution as drafted came from the Republican minority led by the head of the legal division for the Santa Fe railroad—Henry Asp of Guthrie.

Trouble began when W. H. Twine, a black floor leader for the anti-Frantz crowd, climbed onto a chair and moved that Asp be allowed to address the assemblage. The motion "carried with a whoop" and Chairman Twine "so declared." In fear that Asp would make an anti-constitution address and stampede the blacks supporting the Frantz standard (many blacks did not like the constitution anyway), Twine was unceremoniously hauled from his perch and a "Frantz for Governor" banner nailed to the wall.

Asp was brought into the hall amidst a "comingling of

cheers and hisses." The crowd surged toward the rostrum to prevent him from speaking, and Twine "started a fist fight" with a Frantz supporter. "In a second, a dozen guns were flashed, knives were drawn and chairs and tables were swinging in the air. There were a thousand people in the hall and the stampede became general." But for the timely arrival of Bud Ledbetter, with half a dozen policemen who were swinging clubs, "there would likely have been bloodshed."

Bud took the rostrum, waving aloft his six-shooter, and "finally succeeded in bringing order out of chaos." Asp disappeared, and some convention members had the "forethought to secret Twine in a barn until he was given an opportunity to get back to town."

Within twenty minutes, the convention was back in business. "Walter Falwell defeated C. C. Ayers for chairman by a vote of 97 to 60, which exhibited relative strength for Frantz and anti-Frantz sentiment. . . . It was a famous victory for the wing of the party favoring placing in the field of a complete state ticket. . . . Ringing resolutions were passed declaring Frantz for governor and statehood in event the state convention decides to adopt the action." The convention adjourned harmoniously, with "thanks to Ledbetter for saving the day."[6]

With statehood on the horizon, a great concern in Indian Territory was the "woefully congested" criminal docket. There were 400 cases at Muskogee "not even set for trial," 200 in the Wewoka court, and the total of such cases was estimated at 7,000. "If all the cases are taken off the hands of the government by state courts," opined Marshal Bennett, "it will take five years to clean the dockets." The Muskogee press complained: "If the cases are transferred to state courts, as required by the Enabling Act and proposed constitution, those who have charges against them could plead 'no jurisdiction,' according to law, and a case of the United States vs. John Doe could not be tried as the State of Oklahoma vs. John Doe. . . . Some of the best lawyer-members of the constitutional convention have protested this provision on the ground that it would set at liberty all persons against whom indictments have been returned. . . . Among these cases pending are some of the worst criminals in the annals of history, and who, if turned loose, would repeat their operations as soon as they could reach their old haunts."[7]

The constitution went to Washington without this matter being reconsidered, and was submitted to the people of both territories for ratification on September 17. Elections were held on the same date for governor and other state offices, legislature, congressmen, and county and local officers. The constitution was overwhelmingly adopted by a vote of 180,333 to 73,059. The separate prohibition amendment carried 130,361 to 112,258. Democrats won all the principal state offices, including comfortable majorities in both houses of the legislature. Four Democrats and one Republican won the five congressional seats allocated by the Enabling Act. Democrat Charles N. Haskell defeated Republican Frank Frantz for governor, 137,559 votes to 110,292, while C. C. Ross, the Socialist Party nominee, received less than 10,000.

The attorney general in Washington authorized Marshal Bennett to appoint sixty species deputies in different parts of Indian Territory to "forestall lawlessness" until sheriffs of the various counties formed from the Territory could qualify, and until "officially notified that a statehood proclamation had been issued." Ledbetter supervised this deputy operation.[8]

Bells rang and whistles blew throughout the two territories the morning of November 16, when word was telegraphed from Washington that President Roosevelt had formally signed the proclamation of statehood. Just before noon, Governor Haskell was inaugurated at Guthrie before a crowd of thousands. Oklahoma became the fourth state in the nation to be "dry" and the forty-sixth to be admitted to the Union.

Though prohibition legally went into effect when President Roosevelt affixed his signature to the constitution at 10:16 A.M., Governor Haskell gave the saloons in Oklahoma Territory until midnight to dispose of their last drop of beer and whiskey. During those few hours of grace, 500 saloons (forty-six in Oklahoma City alone) closed their doors, and the saloon element had its last fling. Stocks of beer and whiskey were carted away in wagons, buggies, on horseback, and a few automobiles. Drunks roamed the streets, going from one establishment to another. One Oklahoma City company poured thousands of gallons of beer into the gutters and scores of men dashed to the scenes to dip it up in pails before it flowed into the sewer. Brawls, common enough in most towns during the saloon days, were plentiful on that last night and kept local officers and deputy marshals busy. It was almost a week before "dry" Oklahoma quieted down.

Before the day ended, the State Supreme Court convened to organize the judiciary. Through the leadership of Chief Justice Robert L. Williams and enactments of the first state legislature shortly thereafter, a Criminal Court of Appeals, consisting of three members, was created, leaving the Supreme Court with jurisdiction over only civil cases. The new judicial system extended to district, superior, county, municipal, and justice of the peace courts. Law enforcement became the responsibility of sheriffs, chiefs of police, town marshals, and constables.

On the federal level, Oklahoma was divided into a Western District, embracing former Oklahoma Territory, with headquarters at Guthrie, and an Eastern District, embracing the northern, western, central, and southern districts of former Indian Territory, with headquarters at Muskogee. At Guthrie, then U.S. Marshal John R. Abernathy resigned January 13, 1908, leaving Chief Deputy Chris Madsen acting marshal until the appointment on February 11, 1911, of William S. Cade for the Western District.

The greatest disturbance in federal official life was in the Eastern District, now with one set of federal officers where there had been four. Each of the four districts had an average of thirty officials and field deputies—120 in all. District attorneys, their assistants, commissioners, and the U.S. marshals resigned or continued to hold office to the end of their terms. Grosvenor A. Porter, marshal of the Southern District, Indian Territory (a cousin of President Roosevelt), became the United States marshal at Muskogee, his force reduced to a handful of deputies.

Federal work dwindled to routine matters. The days of big manhunting for the government were over.

On November 16, 1907, fifteen federal officials at Muskogee gathered on the steps of the courthouse to be photographed. The occasion was the termination of their jobs at statehood. The group included Marshal Bennett, Deputies Ledbetter, Adams, Coulter, and Paul Williams; U.S. Attorney

Melette and Assistant U.S. Attorney Leekley; and Ceasar Whitmore, long-time courthouse janitor.

Bennett had told the *Muskogee Phoenix* of October 7, 1907: "I am eagerly counting the days when I will go out of office. I am going to rest for several months, then embark in business of some kind in Muskogee. I have all I want of office." In his final report to the Department of Justice, he stated that during his ten years as marshal, he and his deputies had taken 10,455 prisoners. Larceny cases led with a total of 3,420; liquor violations, 2,338; 621 murder cases; 724 assaults to kill.

Bennett engaged in banking and other enterprises until his health became impaired. He died while on a visit to Mineral Wells, Texas, May 27, 1917, and was buried at Muskogee. Praises for his tenure as a lawman, for many years, remained unsung.

Many of his deputies let out of the service at statehood— despite having devoted a great part of their lives to bringing law to Indian Territory—found employment with county governments and municipalities.

Ledbetter was no exception.

Chapter 23

Police Chief:
To Be, or Not to Be

Bud BECAME THE LONE POLICEMAN at Webbers Falls, a railroad town of 500 population on the banks of the Arkansas, twenty-five miles southeast of Muskogee. It was one of the oldest settlements in Muskogee County, named for a rock falls which a century of constant flow of water had gradually worn away until only a ripple marked the point. The Pioneer Trading Company, established many years previous, was one of its most prosperous institutions.

Webbers Falls was a quiet place—too quiet for Ledbetter. "Because of the peaceful nature of his duties, Bud grew restless."[1] In less than two months, he was summoned to Haskell.

Formerly Sawolka (an Indian name meaning "raccoon town"), the name had been changed to Haskell with the coming of the Midland Valley railroad in 1904, in honor of Oklahoma's governor, one of the town's promoters. It had developed on an eighty-acre tract of high prairie in extreme northwestern Muskogee County, halfway between Muskogee and Tulsa. A number of natural gas wells had been drilled, oil discovered, and the rush of oil prospectors and drillers was in full blast.

"The criminal element is taking over," the authorities told Bud. They needed a veteran officer with judgment and bravery to "keep the lid on." Haskell offered excitement to Bud's liking, and he "could not refuse the call." Within a few weeks, he "had the situation in hand."[2]

Bud served as town marshal into the spring of 1908, when the opportunity arose to become chief of police at Muskogee. Because of the political and legal ramifications that followed, this was probably the one big mistake of his career.

Following statehood, Congress had removed restrictions from an additional class of Indian allottees, resulting in millions of acres more in Oklahoma which could be sold and made taxable. Discovery of oil on these lands brought a resurgence of leasing, and the Indian offices in Muskogee were swamped with operators. New business structures and residences were going up everywhere. The city was constructing and enlarging its waterworks and storm sewers. A program of street paving had been launched. The population had increased to more than 14,000.

This growth had also brought more crime and violence. Police Chief Charles Kimsey had been reelected in April 1907, but there was much dissatisfaction with his performance. Rumors of graft and corruption were flying. But business people seemed more interested in making money than in morals, and the city fathers were more concerned with Muskogee still being a city of the second class.

Under provisions of Chapter 29 of Mansfield's Digest of the Statutes of Arkansas, on corporations, put in force in Indian Territory by the Curtis Bill of 1898, cities of the first class comprised a population exceeding 5,000, cities of the second class comprised a population of less than 5,000, but not less than 2,500, which applied at that time to Muskogee. No provision had been made in the Enabling Act or the state constitution for extending in force the laws under which municipal corporations of Indian Territory had been created, organized, and governed. They were agencies of the federal government, and this form of government in Indian Territory at the admission of Oklahoma into the Union ceased to exist. Thus, the laws under which Muskogee held its charter and exercised its municipal powers became inoperative.

Muskogee, as a municipal corporation, would have ceased to exist, except for Section 10 of the Schedule of Oklahoma's constitution. This section provided that all officers of cities and towns heretofore incorporated under the laws in force at the time of statehood "shall perform the duties of their respective offices under the law extended in force in the state, until their successors are elected and qualified in the manner that is or may be provided by law"; and "all valid ordinances now in force . . . shall continue in force until altered, amended or repealed."

Oklahoma's first legislature, on February 20, 1908, had passed an act, approved by the governor, providing that "all cities, towns, and villages and communities of people residing in compact form in this state, having a population of twenty hundred or more, as shown by the special federal census of Oklahoma and Indian Territory, of July 1, 1907, and residing upon land platted into lots and blocks and which were not cities of the first class on November 16, 1907, may become cities of the first class. . . ." The act prescribed a petition containing more than thirty-five percent of the qualified electors within a city, and praying for such an election and the election of city officers as provided by law, to be filed with the governor; prescribed a board of canvassers for such election, how the vote should be canvassed, and "the result certified to the Governor, who, if a majority of votes so cast were in favor . . . shall issue a proclamation within 20 days, declaring such city to be a city of the first class."[3]

Muskogee acted accordingly. Governor Haskell proclaimed the election requested by the petitioners and to fill certain city offices not filled by appointment, as provided by law. Ledbetter filed as the Democratic candidate against Republican Kimsey for chief of police. The election was set for March 24.

The criminal element decided to defeat Bud, "no matter who his opponent was," and a group of gamblers and bootleggers "raised a fund to support their purpose."[4] Mayor J. E. Wyand, apprised of the opposition, announced that he "did not want to be mayor of Muskogee unless he had a council supporting the confidence of the good people," and called on voters to cast their ballots for Ledbetter to assist him in ridding the city of "disreputable officials, law violators, negro repeaters, confidence men, and crooks," making Muskogee "a bigger and better place to live."[5]

During the campaign, several threats were made on Bud's life and the life of Governor Haskell. Nonetheless, the petition prayed for carried with a minimum of objection, Governor Haskell proclaimed Muskogee a first class city, and Bud was elected police chief.

The press was quick to interview Bud about the election threats. "The gangs in the territory have been whipped out now; it is not so dangerous as it used to be," he said. "I've never been shot at from ambush, but there are plenty of men who would shoot me on sight if I gave them a chance. I have run into a good many traps laid for me, but was always lucky enough to back out."

How about his title of "Carry Nation"? How had he become so adept in detecting packages of liquor shipped in by freight or express that his instinct seemed to have developed a sixth sense?

"I can't tell how I know there is liquor in a package, but it is not once out of twenty times that I have opened a box that contained something besides liquor. . . .

"But I can tell you this: It is impossible to bottle whiskey so it will not shake. If you fill the bottles or jugs so full that it will not shake and then cork it up, it will break the bottle. You can cork beer up so it won't rattle, but you can't whiskey."

Did he have a solution for the liquor problem in "dry" Oklahoma?

"I could pick twenty men and keep it out of the entire state. But these would have to be crack men with nothing else to do. I would station a man at the first town inside the state line on every railroad and have him search every freight and express car. This, and a law giving the officers the authority to demand every waybill, would soon break up the shipping by railroad. Of course, there is a good deal of liquor brought in now in wagons and a few automobiles."[6]

Bud took the oath of office on April 6 and began reorganizing and improving police department operations. He kept a desk sergeant on duty day and night so that people would know where to find a policeman when one was needed. The department was more or less self-sustaining—enough revenue being received from fines to pay all expenses—and taxpayers became willing to foot the bill for an extra officer with a patrol wagon outfit.

Many, however, were definitely not ready for "strong liquor law enforcement." As Bud recalled, "I estimated that $65,000 a week was spent on booze in Muskogee. It was illegal, but it was there anyway. . . . On one drive, we cleaned out the town. In one day, I shipped three boxcar loads of confiscated liquor to Guthrie [the state dispensary]. We had everything from Three Star Hennessey to poke-berry red. . . . In another raid, I took 76 barrels of beer from one of the popular parlors. It made a full carload."[7]

Bud also "confiscated large quantities of intoxicating bitters from local druggists." He declared that, whatever their respectability in the community and however prone they were to fill the amen corner in church, they were no better than brush-sulking whiskey peddlers, and that judges and juries should be no respector of persons, but do their duty though the heavens fall.[8]

Things went well for Bud until Charles Kimsey claimed the March election had been illegal and demanded that Bud surrender to him the office of police chief. Bud maintained he had qualified under the law and refused to vacate. Whereupon Kimsey, by the state attorney general, Charles West, filed ouster proceedings in the state supreme court.

The suit asserted that Muskogee was a city of the second class at statehood, its officers regulated and controlled by the laws in force in Indian Territory; that the special election in March was for the purpose of incorporating Muskogee as a city of the first class and continuing current officers to administer its government, but not for electing their successors; that Kimsey was still chief of police under the provisions of Chapter 29 of Mansfield's Digest of the Statutes of Arkansas, and until Muskogee held an election as a city of the first class.[9]

These precepts had already come before the supreme court for construction in the application by the state, on the relation of Adam Kline, for a writ of mandamus to Burril B. Bridges, mayor of Chickasha. The rule announced by the court on March 25, 1908, as to the election of successors of the officers of the city of Chickasha applied to Muskogee.[10] Referring to this rule, and requoting the provisions of the constitution and the act of the state legislature of February 20, the court was of the unanimous opinion that "Charles Kimsey is entitled to the office of chief of police."[11]

The decision, filed September 16, 1908, was cheered by Muskogee's criminal element. But the respite from Bud's raids was short-lived. In the election of 1909, Bud ran for police chief on the law and order ticket, and won. Again, he moved with precision and vigor. Liquor and gambling joints either ceased operations or were raided, and red light districts were closed.

Kimsey continued to be a thorn in Bud's side. This time he brought suit in district court on grounds that "enough citizens had been disenfranchised by the action of the county election board in changing precinct lines the day before the election, to change the result." Bud claimed, "the action of the election board was entirely legal and regular," and delayed the proceedings with a writ of mandamus to the supreme court, in which he attempted to establish the bias and prejudice of the allegations and to disqualify the district judge, supposedly a Kimsey supporter, from trying the case. On May 28, 1910, the supreme court ruled: "The facts do not justify the issuance of the writ prayed for . . . the same is accordingly denied." In December the district court decided in favor of Kimsey.[12]

Bud's attorneys filed notice of appeal, but Bud nixed it. He had been "counted out," as he put it, and was tired of legal hassles. In 1911 he obtained 160 acres with a modern frame home seven miles southeast of Muskogee, got himself a cow, some chickens, a span of mules, and a few farm implements, and announced that he was putting up his guns.

A year later, he was wearing a badge again.

Chapter 24

Sheriff of Muskogee County, and Movie-Making

No sheriff of Muskogee County since statehood had served a full term. R. B. Ramsey, the first, had been indicted by a grand jury for irregularity in office. He was exonerated afterwards and ran a second time, but was defeated. John Wisener, who was appointed to serve out Ramsey's term and later elected, resigned in October 1912, and W. R. Robinson was appointed to serve Wisener's unexpired term.

Meanwhile, lawlessness and the African-American problem were on the rise. At Coweta, twenty miles northwest of Muskogee and too close for comfort, a race riot erupted in 1911. One-third of Coweta's 1,200 population was black.

Saturday afternoon, March 18, a young, white telegraph operator for the Katy railroad named Swazer was walking his girlfriend along the street, when Ed Ruse, a black man, "pushed the girl off the sidewalk into the mud. . . . Swazer gave him a beating." Sunday afternoon Ruse appeared on the streets with a knife, looking for Swazer. "City Marshal Hurl ordered him to give up the knife . . . Ruse attacked Hurl, and Hurl shot him, but not fatally." Ed Suddeth, a black, ran out of a house across the street and "opened fire with an automatic pistol." City Attorney J. D. Beavers, a white candidate for prosecuting attorney of Wagoner County, "was shot through the head and died instant-

159

ly," and two men named Oliver and Thompson were "shot
through the body. All three were bystanders and had taken no
part in the trouble."

The shooting then "became general." Suddeth fled back
into the house and barricaded himself. A white mob riddled the
structure with lead and set it on fire. Suddeth "ran out and was
wounded, but not fatally." He was taken to the railroad station,
a rope around his neck, and swung up on the water tank, but
"cooler heads prevailed and the mob agreed to cut him down
under the promise that he would be legally hanged within thirty days," if he did not die of his wounds. "Deputy Sheriff
Flowers, who had an automobile, endeavored to take him to
Wagoner away from the scene of the crime. As [he] was lifted
into the automobile the mob again broke loose, firing probably
fifty shots into his body."

Blacks arrived from the countryside, "resentful and sullen,"
as tidings of the day reached them. Emissaries headed for sur-
rounding settlements, "swearing to bring in enough negroes to
burn the town off the map." Coweta had no fire protection.
"One negro woman set out for Red Bird, exclusively a negro
town, declaring that she would have all of the town on Coweta
before Monday morning. . . . She was captured by City Marshal
Hurl, but it was rumored that Red Bird negroes already had
learned of the trouble and were on the way."

There were no electric lights in Coweta. Sunday night the
town was in darkness. "White men guarded their homes with
shot-guns and six-shooters, but not enough Winchesters." They
were also "short of ammunition," and afraid to bring their wom-
en to the railroad station to board the last train to Muskogee at
midnight. District Judge W. R. Allen and Sheriff James Long of
Wagoner County called for the state militia. Capt. W. A. Green
of Company F left Muskogee immediately with fifty men, and
deputy sheriffs were sent from Muskogee and Tulsa counties.
"The outbreak was quelled the next day."[1]

On February 14, 1912, Dr. T. A. Scott of Braggs was summoned from his home at 2:00 in the morning, leaving his wife
asleep and alone. A few minutes later, she was "awakened by a
negro bending over her bed." Her attacker held a pillow over
her face as he dragged her onto the porch where she managed

to "break from his grasp and cry for help." Neighbors rushed to her rescue, and the man fled. Deputy sheriffs arrived from Muskogee with bloodhounds and took the trail before daylight. "Almost every man in Braggs and vicinity joined the chase." A black man was arrested, but "officers could not determine that he was the right man."[2]

Three days later, a farmer named Robert Steer was found in his home four miles north of Oktaha, "nearly dead from a beating received during the night." He had sold a load of cotton in Oktaha, and theft of the proceeds was believed to have been the motive. Ira Bruner, a black who had been picking cotton for Steer, surfaced with "more money than usual in his possession," and was arrested by the township constable.[3]

Steer was well-respected around Oktaha. He finally recovered, but his neighbors remained disturbed and angry over the assault.

Other such attacks and racial incidents occurred during 1911-1912, but were not the only reason for citizen disenchantment with Muskogee County's minions of the law. Prohibition had yet to be effectually carried out under state statutes, and the federal government was asked to resort to the "dry blanket" process which had been so unpopular in territorial days.

Samuel Grant Victor had succeeded Grosvenor Porter as U.S. marshal at Muskogee. Victor admitted that "booze dispensation and possession" in Oklahoma was illegal in any of the counties—"even for medicinal or sacramental purposes without obtaining a permit from the War Department"—and promised to make the Eastern District "as dry as simoons on the Sahara." Parson Brannon, who had succeeded federal liquor agent "Pussyfoot" Johnson, cooperated with fifty deputies. During the spring and summer of 1912, they "scoured Muskogee and adjoining counties," spying on the "traffic." More than a dozen big-time bootleggers were hauled into federal courts at Muskogee and Vinita, and Marshal Victor announced that "the work has not yet begun."[4]

W. R. Robinson, for some unknown reason and within weeks after being appointed to succeed John Risener, resigned as sheriff of Muskogee County. The county commissioners asked Ledbetter to serve the remainder of 1912, and his appointment was promptly confirmed. Bud then ran for a full two-year term and was elected by a large majority.

Bud lost no time in naming his official family. Most were former members of the U.S. Marshals service. His first order to his deputies came as no surprise: "The law will be enforced— not any particular law, but every law in the state statutes." They would "play no favorites, or double-cross anybody," and any deputy who winked at the law violator would be disciplined summarily. Racial incidents would be dealt with promptly and effectively. Gambling and the sale of liquor were "the worst forms of evil . . . in a great measure responsible for the commission of other crimes." Those who attempted to engage in such business in Muskogee County could expect rough sledding, and any bootlegger or gambler caught carrying weapons to guard his operations would suffer additional consequences.[5]

Bud adhered to his policies successfully. He suppressed crime and violence, and in cooperation with Marshal Victor and B. A. Enlow, Jr. (who succeeded Victor as marshal in August 1913), he dried up Muskogee County to the satisfaction of the majority of his constituents.

Shortly after his sixty-first birthday in December 1914, he told a reporter: "If I live until January 4, I will be the only sheriff of Muskogee County to serve a full term. I will not run for re-election, and haven't made up my mind what I'll do after I leave office. I expect to make a crop on my farm next year. I'm going to do anything to make an honest livelihood."

He added jokingly: "I'm too old to go on the vaudeville stage—not too old, but not as gay as I once was."[6]

Bud was referring to his recent session with Al Jennings, the ex-bandit he had wounded and captured seventeen years before.

Since his release from prison in 1902, Jennings had cut quite a swath in politics and movie-making. He had reestablished his law practice, locating at Lawton, and married Miss Maude Deaton, a talented musician and graduate of Drake University in Iowa, whose influence he credited with his success in winning back a respectable place in society. In February 1907 President Roosevelt had issued him a "citizenship pardon." He moved his law practice to Oklahoma City and, in 1912, became a candidate for county attorney. "When I was a train robber and outlaw I was a good train robber and outlaw; if you choose me for prosecuting attorney I will be a good prosecuting attorney," he said. Although voters questioned his sincerity, enough of them took his word to give him the Democratic nomination. He lost, however, to D. K. Pope in the general election.

Jennings shrugged off his rejection as another obstacle in his path of reformation. In 1913 he and Will Irwin, a popular writer of the period, co-authored an account of his life entitled *Beating Back,* which was serialized in the *Saturday Evening Post.* The Thanhouser Film Company of New York purchased use of the story for $5,000. Jennings closed his law office and headed East. With Al playing himself and acting as technical advisor, *Beating Back* was completed in the Thanhouser studios and on a rented farm near Ogdensburg, New Jersey. Early in 1914, a New York company published *Beating Back* as a book.

Encouraged by this wide publicity and his creditable showing in the race for county attorney, Jennings sought the Democratic nomination for governor of Oklahoma along with candidates Robert L. Williams and J. B. A. Robertson, a protégé of incumbent Governor Lee Cruce. This time, Jennings pledged himself to honesty in government and law enforcement, noting his "special qualifications" for dealing with prison reform and declaring to crowds across the state: "I will replace men who are now in prison with Oklahoma's crooked politicians." Williams defeated Robertson by a narrow margin, Jennings coming in third with 21,732 votes. In the general election on November 3, Jennings turned his back on Democrats in favor of Republican nominee John Fields, whom Williams narrowly defeated, 100,597 votes to 95,904. Republicans challenged the 4,693 plurality for Williams, charging poll-tampering in sixteen southeastern counties, and Williams was not declared the state's third governor until a week later.

Jennings returned to the theater circuit, proudly displaying his pardon from Roosevelt with the *Beating Back* showings, and lecturing on his favorite topic, "Crime Does Not Pay." He conceived of adding a significant attraction in describing his part in the Spike S ranch battle on stage during his lecture performances.

Ledbetter had not seen *Beating Back,* but understood that

much of the action evolved from the ranch fight. Since he was not a good storyteller and reluctant to recite his exploits, Jennings was to handle the narration while Bud gave an exhibition of his pistol shooting. Bud replied that he was a better shot with a rifle. Whatever the weapon he chose, Jennings would pay him $500 a week. Tempted by the attractive salary offer, Bud said: "I've got a notion to go for it. Think I could get by?" he added, doing a little jig step.[7]

But the veteran lawman reconsidered. He'd had such a hard fight at the Spike S ranch that he always thought the government did wrong in letting Al out of prison after serving so little of his sentence. Furthermore, he had not been impressed with Al's campaign propaganda and thought that if Al was in earnest about reforming, his place would be beneath the redeeming blood and cross of Christ. He refused Jennings' proposition.

Bud was soon glad he had declined. Emmett Dalton, pardoned from the Kansas state penitentiary in 1907, had been traveling the lecture circuit showing films of himself and the Dalton gang committing their well-remembered train and bank holdups in the Oklahoma and Indian territories. On January 1, 1915, Bud received the following letter from Dalton, from Wheeling, West Virginia:

My dear Mr. Ledbetter:

I have just witnessed the exhibition of *Beating Back* by Al Jennings, and I hasten to inquire, what's the chance to borrow the long-tailed Prince Albert coat, boots, star and heavy fierce black mustache you wear in the picture?

It's a good picture but I had one hell of a good laugh when I saw a party impersonating you dressed up as above mentioned, and then knowing you as I do, I could not help think while looking at it, how I would like to hear you express yourself, if you could only see it.

With kindest regards to yourself, family and any friends I may have there, I remain,

As ever, Your friend,
EMMETT DALTON[8]

Some of Bud's friends who had seen the film in the East

told him they were disgusted at how the deeds of the Jennings gang were portrayed as both glamorous and profitable, and deputy marshals as alternately contemptible, blood-thirsty assassins or bungling cowards who stood no chance against Al and his followers. In the Spike S ranch battle, the four outlaws held more than 100 officers at bay, and in a chase scene, Ledbetter was shown streaking across country on a gangling mount, lying low in the saddle and firing promiscuously, his coattails and exaggerated mustache streaming horizontally. Behind him raced the posse with rifle and six-shooters blazing and horses shying left and right at each volley.

Bud was so angered, he remarked that he should have shot Jennings elsewhere than in the leg.

Beating Back also angered Bill Tilghman and Chris Madsen, surviving members of the triumvirate of manhunters famed as Oklahoma's "Three Guardsmen." Heck Thomas had died at Lawton in 1912. Even former U.S. attorneys and several judges were incensed and thought something should be done about the film's lies. E. D. Nix, U.S. marshal for Oklahoma Territory during the heyday of the Bill Doolin and Al Jennings gangs, now resided in St. Louis, dealing in bonds, stocks, and investments. Nix agreed to provide the initial capital for a dramatic picture play that would show the present generation the true sordidness of outlaw life, how the Doolin and Jennings gangs were pursued and destroyed, and be beneficial to Oklahoma instead of detrimental. The Eagle Film Company was incorporated at Oklahoma City, with Nix as president, Tilghman as vice-president and treasurer in charge of production, and Madsen secretary.

The company, with a corps of actors to impersonate well-known desperados, assembled at Tilghman's hometown of Chandler on January 18, 1915. Tilghman, Madsen, and Nix and former U.S. District Attorney Caleb R. Brooks played themselves in the film. Local residents served in posses. Some of the scenes were shot on Tilghman's Bell Cow ranch north of Chandler and along the railroad at nearby Harrah, but most were filmed on location. Ingalls, site of the celebrated battle in which three deputy U.S. marshals died at the hands of the Doolin gang in 1893; the cave on Deer Creek at its confluence with the Cimarron; the Dunn ranch southeast of Ingalls; and other hideouts in Osage and Creek nations became important settings. At Eureka Springs, Arkansas, Tilghman enacted for the cameraman his singlehanded capture of Bill Doolin. At Guthrie, he staged Doolin's escaped in July 1896, and the subsequent death of the bandit chief in August, at Lawson. Finally, the company spent several days filming the Spike S ranch battle and capture of the Jennings gang, under the direction of Ledbetter, who acted his own part.

The *Times-Democrat* of February 10 noted Bud's return to Muskogee, adding: "Former Sheriff Ledbetter is satisfied that the moral effect of the movie will be good, since there was no one killed before the public—that is, in his part of the picture."

The production consisted of four sets of reels, about 6,000 feet of film to the set, the raw material and finishing work costing approximately $10,000, and was titled *The Passing of the Oklahoma Outlaws*. Previewed at Chandler on May 25, people from throughout the area packed the Odeon Theater until after midnight. Hundreds more were thrilled and edified by its inaugural exhibition at the Overholser Theater in Oklahoma City on June 10. Thence, the feature went over the country as a road attraction, Tilghman, Nix, and Madsen working with one set of reels each and, in keeping with the tradition of the time, lecturing from the theater stage at each showing. One set was kept at Oklahoma City headquarters for use of the press and route agent.

The Passing of the Oklahoma Outlaws, with Bud Ledbetter, played the Broadway Theater at Muskogee the last week in June. Huge crowds turned out to witness the performance of their former sheriff. "Prices were 20 cents for the Lower Floor, 10 cents for Balcony. . . . This is one picture that is typical of the gallantry and heroism of officers in early Oklahoma days. . . . It shows to the people who can hardly conceive the reality that well-known men, who were agents in history-making in this state, really appear in this marvelous photographic reproduction of Oklahoma's campaign to exterminate criminals of the reckless and desperate class." The citizens of Muskogee considered their hero Ledbetter "a famous movie star."[9]

In September Nix returned to his investments in St. Louis. At Christmas time, Madsen also quit the circuit and retired at

Guthrie to write his autobiography. Tilghman bought out his partners and for the next several years toured with the film from the Gulf Coast to Michigan, from Colorado to California. He did good business until "cowboy" stars took over the theater screen and his seventy years seemed unequal to the grueling schedule. In 1924 he accepted a job policing the oil boomtown of Cromwell, Oklahoma, and was slain by a drunken prohibition agent he had trusted.

Al Jennings had long since closed his *Beating Back* operation on the West Coast, playing bit parts in a number of Western movies before retiring on a chicken ranch in southern California. He died in 1962.

Chapter 25

---

100 Battles and
Never Scratched

Ledbetter followed a quiet farm life until 1917, when a group of Okmulgee citizens prevailed on him to do his usual job of cleaning up the town. He left the cultivation of his crops to his son George, and responded like an old fire horse to a new conflagration.

The excitement over the Glenpool discoveries had spread to Okmulgee with strikes made in 1906, and ten miles northeast at Bald Hill, in 1908. Since 1912, other strikes had been made in deeper sands, creating a diversion of oil operators northwestward to within six miles of Beggs. Okmulgee was the supply center and a site on the eight-inch line of the Gulf Production Company, which carried seven million barrels of crude annually, with tankage and pump stations, from the Tulsa–Glenpool area to Port Arthur, Texas, refineries. Gamblers and whiskey peddlers thrived, and chislers, thieves, and punks were a dime a dozen, making the city a hotbed of crime on the eve of World War I.

Bud never talked about his work at Okmulgee, and journalists recorded nothing of his activities, except "the city hired him as a plainclothes detective on the police force." He served until after the war years, virtually a one-man vice squad, and "needless to say, he got things straightened out."[1]

Bud returned to farming in 1922, in time to help George

with the spring planting. He was almost seventy. That summer he was called upon to head posses of much younger men in their hunt for the slayers of Deputy Sheriff Homer Teaff. Many stories were told about how he kept up with the best of them, sleeping on the ground at night, braving storms and lack of food, until the killers were captured.

It was election time in Muskogee County and many of his friends urged him to run again on the Democratic ticket for sheriff. Bud declined. He was a family man, a grandfather. "I'm too old, " he said, "and people are getting tired of hearing about me."

"Try it and find out," his friends advised.

Bud won the August primary in a walk. His Republican opponent in the November election was Joe Wilks, a World War I veteran. It was youth versus old age. But it was Bud's record of public service, "characterized by marked devotion to duty and efficiency in the discharge of the tasks which had devolved upon him," that gave him a majority of more than 3,000 votes. The confidence and respect the people expressed for him that day made him as proud as when he received his first appointment as a young deputy sheriff in Arkansas.

Bud took office on January 2, 1923. Though his seventy years were "bearing down on him" he continued his never-ending war on thieves, hijackers, murderers, and moonshiners. Newspapers were replete with such headlines as "Uncle Bud's Boys Seize Four Stills"; "Overnight, Deputy Sheriffs Clean Up on Moonshine Plants"; "Criminals Seek Better Climes"; "Veteran Sheriff Hums 'Day by Day, Muskogee County is Growing Better.'" This time, Bud served two terms, until 1928, when his common sense told him to put away his guns for good.[3]

Rugged lawman that he was, Ledbetter had a compassion unusual for a person who had dealt with the criminal element almost half a century. He often posted bail for a wrongdoer he believed "had good in him," and even helped a criminal's family. Once he obtained furlough for a convict to be at the deathbed and funeral of his father. One story not generally circulated, according to his granddaughter, Mrs. Earl Corliss, was the occasion he posted bond for an alleged preacher who skipped, costing him $500.[4]

Many doubted that Bud had a conscience. This was dispelled on December 16, 1922, when former U.S. Marshal Morton Rutherford, who had given him his first deputy's commission in Indian Territory, was fatally injured in an automobile accident. Rutherford's body was laid out in an upstairs room of his home in Muskogee. "The grizzled Ledbetter . . . knelt at the bier of his friend and benefactor and wept like a child."[5]

Bud settled down with his wife "to enjoy life" in their old home at 415 West Southside Boulevard, leaving his farm in charge of George and family. He went there frequently "just to putter around and pet and groom the livestock," and boasted of having "the best team of mules in Muskogee County." He became a venerable figure on the streets, in the courthouse, in the federal building, and at conventions of the Oklahoma Sheriffs and Peace Officers Association, of which he was a charter member and co-founder. He was also a member of the Ex-Deputy U.S. Marshals Association—men still living who had been commissioned in different districts of Indian Territory—and for years had been a faithful follower of the teachings and purposes of the Masonic fraternity. He loved to visit Vinita, Okmulgee, and other towns where he had served as a city officer, and made a couple of trips to his old haunts in Arkansas. Once asked if he did not get tired of shaking hands with so many people he knew, he replied: "Old friends are precious to me. . . . I've shook hands with as many as 2,000 people in one day." But when plied for stories of his experiences, he remained reticent. "Not that they were kept secret," Mrs. Corliss said, "merely that he never discussed them at home, and nothing was made of it."[6]

Bud's retirement was marred in 1930 by the loss of his faithful wife of fifty-six years. He was never the same afterwards. He went to live with George, visited less in Muskogee and about the state, but kept physically active.

Bud seldom rode from the farm to the city, preferring to walk instead. On one such trip, in mid-April 1933, he stopped at a roadside store, and fell, breaking two ribs under his left arm. The excuse he gave a *Tulsa World* reporter four weeks later: "I wasn't feeling as well as usual; my heart must have missed a beat. . . . I've been in bed, but I'm not sick."

The reporter found him "mentally alert as ever . . . keeping abreast of current events." He had "definite opinions" about the national scene, and didn't mind expressing them. He believed President Franklin Delano Roosevelt, inaugurated in March, "to be the greatest man in the world today." An estimated one-third of the nation's labor force was out of work. Many who had jobs were working for as little as ten cents an hour. Malnutrition and starvation in many parts of the country had become facts of life. Roosevelt was putting into effect major pieces legislation to remedy the problems, and trying to lift the nation's morale with encouraging radio speeches, called "fireside chats."

"He had the whole country back of him in the election," Bud said. "Even if the Democrats hadn't voted for him, the Republicans would have. . . ." But he disagreed with the measure Roosevelt had signed into law on March 22 to legalize beer and wine with a maximum alcoholic content of 3.2 percent by weight. "The tax of $5 per barrel, or 31 gallons, may bring in much needed revenue, but it isn't worth it. . . . I know people say that bootlegging is bad—that's been shown by the gangster and his methods in Chicago—but it is not as bad as the saloon."[7]

He was sorely disappointed December 5, when national prohibition was repealed as Utah became the 36th state to ratify the 21st Amendment of the Constitution.

Bud appeared hale and hearty on December 15, 1934, when he celebrated his eighty-second birthday, sitting by the fire in his farm home, chatting with several old friends and a *Phoenix* staff writer who attended the occasion. He was coaxed into giving a "descriptive account" of his fight at Blackstone Switch. "It was one of my tightest spots, " he concluded, adding that "one well-directed shot from his trusty rifle" had made a preacher out of Texas Jack. And that was as much reminiscing as the reporter got from him. Informed that his exploits were "half-legendary" because of his refusals to state whether stories told about him were actual or not, he remarked: "I plan one day to write my memoirs."[8]

Whether or not Bud seriously considered putting his experiences in a book, he must have known he already had waited too long. He was suffering from heart disease December 15, 1936, when he celebrated his eighty-fourth birthday with family and friends at Sapulpa and Shamrock, Oklahoma. His daughter, Mrs. Dolly Young of Kansas City, was unable to attend and sent her best wishes. A few days later, George took him to the Muskogee General Hospital.

Bud objected to hospital confinement. During the early months of 1937 he was shuttled to and from his farm for treatment. Doctors "marveled at his resistance to his heart affliction," and people all over Oklahoma followed the newspaper accounts of his fight for life. "Frequently he was reported as sinking, but each time his remarkable stamina kept him from giving up." At the end of June, he "took to his bed . . . critically ill." On July 7 he lapsed into a coma, was rushed to the hospital, and was never fully conscious afterwards. The aged lawman died peacefully at 10:14 P.M., Thursday, July 8, his son George and daughter Dolly at his bedside.[9]

Muskogee stores closed and public offices suspended services for the funeral on July 10. Peace officers from Arkansas and throughout Oklahoma came to pay homage. The Muskogee sheriff's office and police department, with the exception of three men on duty, attended in force, as well as a staff of United States marshals.

Some time before his death, Bud had visited with one longtime friend, State Senator Gid Graham of Collinsville. The two old-timers had sat up all night, talking, and made a pact: the one who lived the longest would deliver a eulogy at the other's last rites.

Graham kept the promise. Before 1,500 persons in the Muskogee Municipal Auditorium, he praised Ledbetter as one who "made Oklahoma a safe place where honest men could raise a family," and quoted Ledbetter telling him, in their all-night conversation, his conception of heaven: "It is not a place where the streets are paved with gold; my hope of the hereafter is the Indian's dream. I hope I may walk beside a stream, look into the trees, and hear the birds, with no sighs, no trouble, no malice." Graham concluded: "I am proud to have known this man whose three traits of character were kindness, courage and rugged honesty."[10]

Officers who knew Bud Ledbetter best estimated that he had killed or seriously wounded twenty-two men. More certain-

Notes

Chapter 1

1. For birth and early life of James Franklin Ledbetter in Madison County and his migration to Johnson County, Arkansas, see John D. Benedict, *Muskogee and Northeastern Oklahoma* (The S. J. Clarke Publishing Company, Chicago, 1922), Vol. II, 460-463; David Y. Thomas, Editor, *Arkansas and Its People* (American Historical Society, New York, 1930), Vol. II, 382, 724-725, 738-739; "'Bud' Ledbetter, Pioneer Officer," *Muskogee Daily Phoenix*, July 9, 1937; Helen Starr and O. E. Hill, *Footprints in the Indian Nation* (Hoffman Printing Company, Inc., Muskogee, Oklahoma, 1974), 75; C. W. "Dub" West, *Persons and Places in Indian Territory* (Muskogee Publishing Company, Muskogee, Oklahoma, 1974), 123—reprinted by author in *Outlaws and Peace Officers of Indian Territory* (Muskogee Printing Company, Muskogee, Oklahoma, 1987), 104-105; Lonnie E. Underhill and Daniel F. Littlefield, Jr., "James F. Ledbetter, Frontier Lawman," *Red River Valley Historical Review*, Vol. 1, No. 4, Winter 1974, 369-370.

2. For Ledbetter's ax-handle performance and tenure as town marshal, see *Tulsa Daily World*, December 15, 1936; C. H. McKennon, "On the Side of the Law," *Tulsa Daily World*, November 5, 1961, and *Iron Men: A Saga of the Deputy United States Marshals Who Rode the Indian Territory* (Doubleday and Company, Garden City, New York, 1967), 73; Starr and Hill, *op. cit.*, 76; West, *Persons and Places, op. cit.*, 123-124, and *Outlaws and Peace Officers, op. cit.*, 105.

3. Benedict, *op. cit.*, 460; McKennon, "On the Side of the Law," *op. cit.;* West, *Persons and Places, op. cit.*, 124, and *Outlaws and Peace Officers," op. cit.*, 105.

Chapter 2

1. *History of Northwest Arkansas. History of Benton, Washington, Carroll, Madison, Crawford, Franklin and Sebastian Counties* (Goodspeed Publishing Company, Chicago, 1889), 628.

2. Holland's escape, recapture, and hanging at Ozark are detailed in Lon R. Stansbery, "Bud Ledbetter, Scourge of Criminals. Veteran Peace Officer Relentless in Pursuit." *Tulsa Daily World,* January 24, 1937.

3. Reports of the Mulberry episode, the apprehension and conviction of the killers of Conductor Cain, and their execution at Clarksville appear in the *Johnson County Herald,* March 9 through June 29, 1883.

See also McKennon, *Iron Men, op. cit.,* 69, 74, 75-78; Starr and Hill, *op. cit.,* 77.

Chapter 3

1. Judge R. L. Williams, "The Judicial History of Oklahoma" (Proceedings of the Fifth Annual Meeting of the Oklahoma Bar Association, Oklahoma City, December 21-22, 1911), 126-127; Roy Gittinger, *The Formation of the State of Oklahoma, 1803-1906* (University of California Press, Berkeley, 1917), 180; Grant Foreman, "Oklahoma's First Court," *Chronicles of Oklahoma,* Vol. XIII, No. 4, December 1935, 457.

2. U.S. Statutes at Large, 50th Congress, Session II, Vol. 25, chap. 333, sections 1-2, 5-8; Vinita *Indian Chieftain,* March 7, 1889; S. W. Harman, *Hell on the Border: He Hanged Eighty-Eight Men* (The Phoenix Publishing Company, Fort Smith, Arkansas, 1898), 53-57.

3. U.S. Statutes at Large, 51st Congress, Session I, Vol. 26, chap. 182, sections 31-34, 36, 41; Roy M. Johnson, compiler, *Oklahoma History, South of the Canadian* (The S. J. Clarke Publishing Company, Chicago, 1925), Vol. I, 158-159.

4. Judge Williams, *op. cit.,* 128; Johnson, *op. cit.,* 159.

Chapter 4

1. For the founding and growth of Vinita and Ledbetter's introduction to the town, see Benedict, *op. cit.,* 658-663; H. E. Ridenhour interview, *Indian-Pioneer History,* Oklahoma Historical Society, Vol. 113, 402-410; O. B. Campbell, *Vinita, I.T., The Story of a Frontier Town of the Cherokee Nation, 1871-1907* (Oklahoma Publishing Company, Oklahoma City, 1969), 1-3; "Vinita Schedules Centennial Party," *Tulsa Daily World,* July 31, 1971.

2. Vinita *Indian Chieftain,* July 26, 1894.

3. Fort Smith *Elevator,* April 17, 1891.

Chapter 5

1. Stansbery, "Bud Ledbetter, Scourge of Criminals," *op. cit.*

2. Nathaniel (Texas Jack) Reed interview, *Indian-Pioneer History,* Oklahoma Historical Society, Vol. 41, 307-311; *The Life of Texas Jack: Eight Years a Criminal, 41 Years Trusting in God* (By Himself, Tulsa, Oklahoma, 1936) 3-14; Glenn Shirley, "The Bungled Job at Blackstone Switch," *True West,* Vol. 13, No. 2, May-June 1966.

3. *Ibid.*

4. Reed interview, *op. cit.,* 310-311; *The Life of Texas Jack, op. cit.,* 16-17.

5. Stansbery, "Bud Ledbetter, Scourge of Criminals," *op. cit.*

6. Vinita *Indian Chieftain,* November 14, 1894; *Muskogee Phoenix,* November 21, 1894; Ardmore *State Herald,* November 22, 1894; Reed interview, *op. cit.,* 311; Stansbery, "Bud Ledbetter, Scourge of Criminals," *op. cit.*

7. *The Life of Texas Jack, op. cit.*, 18-19; Shirley, "The Bungled Job at Blackstone Switch," *op. cit.*

8. Fort Smith, Arkansas dispatch, November 13, *Daily Oklahoman*, November 15, 1894; Vinita *Indian Chieftain*, November 15, 1894; Ardmore *State Herald*, November 22, 1894.

9. *Ibid.; The Life of Texas Jack, op. cit.*, 21.

10. Vinita *Indian Chieftain*, November 15, 1894; Ardmore *State Herald*, November 22, 1894.

11. *The Life of Texas Jack, op. cit.*, 22-25.

12. Harman, *op. cit.*, 373.

Chapter 6

1. Fort Smith Arkansas dispatch, November 13, *Daily Oklahoman*, November 15, 1894.

2. Vinita *Indian Chieftain*, December 13, 1894.

3. *Ibid.;* Harman, *op. cit.*, 451-452.

4. Vinita *Indian Chieftain*, December 27, 1894.

5. Harman, *op. cit.*, 373.

6. U.S. Statutes at Large, 53rd Congress, Session III, Vol. 28, chap. 145, sections 1, 2, 4, 11; Judge Williams, *op. cit.*, 129-130; Benedict, *op. cit.*, 386; Johnson, compiler, *op. cit.*, 159-160.

7. Harman, *op. cit*, 60-63.

8. Benedict, *op. cit.*, 369-370; Jerry Rand, "Samuel Morton Rutherford," *Chronicles of Oklahoma*, Vol. XXX, No. 2, Summer 1952.

9. Nathaniel (Texas Jack) Reed interview, *op. cit.*, 312.

10. *Ibid.*

11. Harman, *op. cit.*, 374.

12. Stansbery, "Bud Ledbetter, Scourge of Criminals," *op. cit.*

13. Vinita *Indian Chieftain*, August 8, 1895; *Muskogee Phoenix*, August 15, 1895; Harman, *op. cit.*, 373-374.

14. *Muskogee Phoenix*, August 22, 1895.

15. Vinita *Indian Chieftain*, August 29, 1895; Fort Smith *Elevator*, August 30, 1895.

16. *Muskogee Phoenix*, August 29, 1895.

17. *Ibid.*, September 13, 1895.

18. *Muskogee Phoenix*, September 19 and 26, 1895; Vinita *Indian Chieftain*, September 26, 1895; *Oklahoma State Capital*, October 17, 1895.

19. *Buz Luckey v. United States*, 163 U.S. 162, 16 Sup. Crt. Reporter 1203; Fort Smith *Elevator*, January 31, 1896.

20. Harman, *op. cit.*, 454.

21. *Oklahoma State Capital*, September 1, 1896.

22. *Dyer v. United States*, 164 U.S. 704, 17 Sup. Crt. Reporter 993.

23. Harman, *op. cit.*, 376-378.

24. *The Life of Texas Jack, op. cit.*, 36; Shirley, "The Bungled Job at Blackstone Switch," *op. cit.*

25. " 'Bud' Ledbetter, Pioneer Officer," *op. cit.*

Chapter 7

1. *Muskogee Phoenix,* August 8, 1895; Stansbery, "Bud Ledbetter, Scourge of Criminals," *op. cit.*

2. *Ibid.*

3. *Muskogee Phoenix,* August 8, 1895.

4. *Ibid.*

5. *Ibid.,* also August 15, 1895.

6. Harman, *op. cit.,* 499-500.

7. *Muskogee Phoenix,* August 15, 1895.

8. *Ibid.;* Ardmore *State Herald,* August 22, 1895; *Oklahoma Daily Times-Journal,* August 24, 1895; Fort Smith *Elevator,* August 30, 1895.

Chapter 8

1. Lon R. Stansbery, *The Passing of the 3-D Ranch* (privately printed, Tulsa, Oklahoma, 1930), 32.

2. Lon R. Stansbery, "Bud Ledbetter, Pioneer G-Man of the West," *Tulsa Daily World,* May 21, 1937.

3. *Ibid.; Oklahoma State Capital,* August 9, 1895; Vinita *Indian Chieftain,* March 12, 1896.

4. *Daily Oklahoman,* June 20, 1894.

5. For accounts of the expedition against the Turner gang, see Stansbery, "Bud Ledbetter, Pioneer G-Man of the West," *op. cit.;* William Frank Jones interview, *Indian-Pioneer History,* Oklahoma Historical Society, Vol. 6, 26-28, and Jones, *The Experiences of a Deputy U.S. Marshal of the Indian Territory* (privately printed, Tulsa, Oklahoma, 1937), 5.

6. Fort Smith *Elevator,* October 16, 1896; Bill Hoge, "Oologah Oozings," *Tulsa Sunday World Magazine,* August 19, 1956; Olevia E. Myers, "Two Sides of the Green Boys," *Old West,* Vol. 10, No. 4, Summer 1974.

7. Hoge, *op. cit.;* S. R. Lewis interview, *Indian-Pioneer History,* Oklahoma Historical Society, Vol. 78, 258-259.

8. *Ibid.*

9. S. R. Lewis interview, *op. cit.*

10. Fort Smith *Elevator,* October 16, 1896; S. R. Lewis interview, *op. cit.,* 260; Hoge, *op. cit.*; Myers, *op. cit.*

11. S. R. Lewis interview, *op. cit.,* 261-262; Hoge, *op. cit.*; Myers, *op. cit.*

12. *Ibid.*

13. Vinita *Indian Chieftain,* October 15, 1896; S. R. Lewis interview, *op. cit.,* 263; Ed Sunday interview, *Indian-Pioneer History,* Oklahoma Historical Society, Vol. 46, 89.

14. Vinita *Indian Chieftain,* December 3, 1896.

Chapter 9

1. Benedict, *op. cit.,* 386.

2. Harman, *op. cit.,* 66.

3. U.S. Statutes at Large, 55th Congress, Session I, Vol. 30, chap. 3, 83; Harman, *op. cit.,* 65-66.

4. U.S. Statutes at Large, 55th Congress, Session II, Vol. 30, chap. 109, 506-507; Harman, *op. cit.,* 66.

5. Judge Williams, *op. cit.*, 130-131; Benedict, *op. cit.* 386, 389; Johnson, compiler, *op. cit.*, 160-161; J. Stanley Clark, "The Career of John R. Thomas," *Chronicles of Oklahoma*, Vol. LII, No. 2, Summer 1974, 163.

6. Benedict, *op. cit.*, 389-390; E. Dixon Larson and Al Ritter, "Leo E. Bennett, Indian Territory Pioneer and Lawman," *Oklahoma State Trooper*, Spring 1995.

7. The crime and capture of K. B. Brooks is detailed in *Muskogee Phoenix*, June 30, 1898, and Harman, *op. cit.*, 712-713.

See also Stansbery, "Bud Ledbetter, Pioneer G-Man of the West," *op. cit.*; Jones, *The Experiences of a Deputy U.S. Marshal of the Indian Territory, op. cit.*, 40.

8. Stansbery, "Bud Ledbetter, Pioneer G-Man of the West," *op. cit.*

Chapter 10

1. For the early life of Al and Frank Jennings and formation of the Jennings gang, see Glenn Shirley, *West of Hell's Fringe: Crime, Criminals and the Federal Peace Officer in Oklahoma Territory, 1889-1907* (University of Oklahoma Press, Norman, 1978), 384-391.

Brief summaries appear in *Muskogee Phoenix*, December 9, 1897; McKennon, *Iron Men, op. cit.*, 197-198; Charles W. Mooney, *Localized History of Pottawatomie County, Oklahoma to 1907* (Privately printed, Midwest City, Oklahoma, 1971), 303; Starr and Hill, *op. cit.*, 81-83.

2. Al Jennings and Will Irwin, *Beating Back* (The Munson Book Company, Toronto. D. Appleton and Company, New York, 1914), 155-156.

3. *Jennings v. United States*, Indian Territory Reports: Cases Determined in the United States Court of Appeals for the Indian Territory, Vol. II, 675.

4. *Jennings v. United States, op. cit.*, 674.

5. *Muskogee Phoenix*, December 9, 1897; *Jennings v. United States, op. cit.*, 675, 682.

Chapter 11

1. *Jennings v. United States, op. cit.*, 672, 682-683; C. H. McKennon, "When Marshals and Outlaws Shot It Out," *Tulsa Daily World*, January 15, 1961.

2. For details of the Spike S ranch battle, see *Jennings v. United States, op. cit.*, 672-673, 683-684; "The Jennings Jerked," *Muskogee Phoenix*, December 9, 1897; Ledbetter interview, *Eufaula Republican*, August 16, 1912; McKennon, "When Marshals and Outlaws Shot It Out," *op. cit.*; Shirley, *West of Hell's Fringe, op. cit.*, 408-410.

3. Final pursuit and capture of the Jennings gang described in Muskogee, I.T. dispatch, December 7, *Guthrie Daily Leader*, December 8, 1897; Muskogee, I.T. dispatch, December 8, *Oklahoma State Capital*, December 8, 1897; "The Jennings Jerked," *op. cit.*

4. "The Jennings Jerked," *op. cit.*

5. Starr and Hill, *op. cit.*, 85.

6. Statement of Jackson Thompson in Jones, *The Experiences of A Deputy U.S. Marshal in the Indian Territory, op. cit.*, 33-34.

7. Vinita *Indian Chieftain*, December 30, 1897.

8. *Muskogee Phoenix*, February 24, 1898.

9. *Ibid.*

10. *Ibid.*

11. *Ibid.*, March 10, 1898.

12. *Daily Oklahoman,* June 3, 1898; *Muskogee Phoenix,* June 9, 1898.

13. *Muskogee Phoenix,* June 2, 1898; *Jennings v. United States, op. cit.,* 672-673, 688.

14. *In re Jennings,* 118 Federal Reporter 479-480; *Oklahoma State Capital,* February 16-18, 1899; *Daily Oklahoman,* February 17-18, 1899.

15. *In re Jennings,* 118 Federal Reporter 479-481.

16. Trials and execution of Brooks and Whitefield detailed in *Muskogee Phoenix,* April 28, May 5 and 26, June 30, and July 7, 1898; Harman, *op. cit.,* 710-713; John Bartlett Meserve, "From Parker to Poe," *Chronicles of Oklahoma,* Vol. XVI, No. 1, March 1938; Clark, *op. cit.,* 163.

17. Ledbetter interview, *Eufaula Republican, op. cit.*

Chapter 12

1. Telegrams quoted in *Muskogee Phoenix,* April 28, 1898. See also Benedict, *op. cit.,* 277 Clark, *op. cit.,* 171; Grant Foreman, *Muskogee, The Biography of An Oklahoma Town* (University of Oklahoma Press, Norman, 1943), 89.

2. *Muskogee Phoenix,* quoted in Clark, *op. cit.,* 172.

3. *Muskogee Phoenix,* May 12, 1898.

4. *Ibid.*

5. *Ibid.*, May 19, 1898.

6. *Ibid.*

7. *Ibid.*

8. *Ibid.*, April 14, 1898.

9. *Ibid.*, May 5, 1898.

10. *Ibid.*, May 19, 1898.

11. *Ibid.*, May 26, 1898.

12. U.S. Statutes at Large, 55th Cong., Session II, Vol. 30, chap. 517, sections 26 and 29; Harman, *op. cit.,* 66-67.

13. Harry H. Adams interview, *Indian-Pioneer History,* Oklahoma Historical Society, Vol. 99, 34-35.

14. *Ibid.*, 36-43. Interview reprinted in Notes and Documents as "The Brush Court in Indian Territory," *Chronicles of Oklahoma,* Vol. XLVI, No. 2, Summer 1968, 201-205.

15. *Muskogee Phoenix,* February 3 and 10, 1898.

16. *Ibid.*, October 6, 1898.

17. *Ibid.*, and October 13, 1898.

Chapter 13

1. Muskogee, I.T. dispatch, May 17, *Daily Oklahoman,* May 18, 1899.

2. Muskogee, I.T. dispatch, August 4, *Daily Oklahoman,* August 5, 1899.

3. Judge Williams, *op. cit.,* 134; Joseph A. Gill, Jr., "Judge Joseph Albert Gill, 1854-1933," *Chronicles of Oklahoma,* Vol. XII, No. 3, September 1934, 375-376.

4. Washington, D.C. dispatch, January 26, *Oklahoma State Capital,* January 27, 1901.

5. Washington, D.C. dispatch, February 7, *Oklahoma State Capital,* February 8, 1901.

Chapter 14

1. "Oklahoma 'Six-Gun' Legends," *Tulsa Tribune,* July 9, 1937.

2. Vinita *Indian Chieftain,* April 4, 1901.

3. *Ibid.,* November 14, 1901.

4. Judge Williams, *op. cit.,* 134; Benedict, *op. cit.,* 393-394; Benjamin J. Martin, "Charles W. Raymond, 1858-1939," *Chronicles of Oklahoma,* Vol. XVII, No. 3, September 1939, 461-462; Clark, *op. cit.,* 173-174, 177.

5. *Johnson County* (Arkansas) *Herald,* February 7, 1902, and June 19, 1903.

6. *Ibid.;* Oklahoma State Capital, February 15, 1902.

7. *Johnson County* (Arkansas) *Herald,* June 19, 1903.

8. 33 U.S. Statutes at Large 245; Judge Williams, *op. cit.,* 134; Meserve, *op. cit.,* 94.

9. Muskogee, I.T. dispatch, August 26, *Daily Oklahoman,* August 27, 1902.

10. Vinita, I.T. dispatch, September 3, *Daily Oklahoman,* September 3, 1902.

Chapter 15

1. Freda Gold, " 'Best' Deputy Marshal Will Begin 50th Year," *Tulsa Daily World,* June 29, 1952, and "Marshal to Give Up Badge After 50 Years of Service," *Tulsa Daily World,* October 24, 1952; C. H. McKennon, "There Was A Stillness, A Still and Lawmen," *Tulsa Daily World,* August 25, 1968.

2. C. H. McKennon, "Oklahoma's Long-Time Marshal," *The West,* Vol. 10, No. 6, May 1969. (Cottle served as deputy marshal at Wewoka until November 13, 1904, then was transferred to Muskogee. In February 1906 he was transferred to Ardmore. He returned to Muskogee in November 1907 and stayed there until transferred to Tulsa in 1929, where he retired after fifty years of service on October 31, 1952).

3. Muskogee, I.T. dispatch, November 18, *Stillwater Gazette,* November 26, 1903.

4. Muskogee, I.T. dispatch, January 12, *Daily Oklahoman,* January 12, 1904.

5. 33 U.S. Statutes at Large 573; Judge Williams, *op. cit.,* 134-135; Benedict, *op. cit.,* 394; Johnson, compiler, *op. cit.,* 163.

6. Muskogee, I.T. dispatch, May 1, *Oklahoma State Capital,* May 3, 1904; Muskogee, I.T. dispatch, May 19, *Oklahoma State Capital,* May 20, 1904.

Chapter 16

1. "How the Creek Indians Lost Millions of Dollars: Civil War Results Still Apparent—Indians Once Owned Slaves Who Gobbled Up the Best of the Lands," Muskogee, I.T. dispatch, April 25, Stillwater *Advance-Democrat,* May 5, 1904; Benedict, *op. cit.,* 228-229; Col. Clarence B. Douglas, "Bud Ledbetter's One-Man Race Riot," *Daily Oklahoman,* April 5, 1936; Foreman, *op. cit.,* 120.

2. Muskogee, I.T. dispatch, April 3, *Daily Oklahoman,* April 3, 1902.

3. *Muskogee Phoenix,* August 21, 1902; Muskogee, I.T. dispatch, August 22, *Daily Oklahoman,* August 24, 1902.

4. Tulsa, I.T. dispatch, November 12, *Daily Oklahoman,* November 13, 1902.

5. Muskogee, I.T. dispatch, May 5, *Oklahoma State Capital,* May 6, 1903.

6. Muskogee, I.T. dispatch, May 6, *Oklahoma State Capital,* May 7, 1903.

7. Paden, I.T. dispatch, June 19, *Daily Oklahoman,* June 20, 1903.

8. Muskogee, I.T. dispatch, May 26, *Daily Oklahoman,* May 27, 1904.

9. Muskogee, I.T. dispatch, July 4, *Daily Oklahoman,* July 5, 1904.

10. Wewoka, I.T. dispatch, July 5, *Daily Oklahoman,* July 6, 1904.

11. Holdenville, I.T. dispatch, July 7, *Daily Oklahoman,* July 8, 1904.

12. Muskogee, I.T. dispatch, November 28, *Daily Oklahoman,* November 29, 1904.

13. Muskogee, I.T. dispatch, December 3, *Daily Oklahoman,* December 4, 1904.

14. Eufaula, I.T. dispatch, December 5, *Daily Oklahoman,* December 6, 1904; Eufaula *Indian Journal,* December 9, 1904.

15. Eufaula *Indian Journal,* December 1, 1905.

16. Ltr. Carl Fink (nephew) to Glenn Shirley, May 8, 1961.

17. *Tulsa Democrat,* December 26, 1904.

18. McKennon, "There Was A Stillness, A Still and Lawmen," *op. cit.,* and "Oklahoma's Long-Time Marshal," *op. cit.*

See also West, *Persons and Places in Indian Territory, op. cit.* 131, and *Outlaws and Peace Officers of Indian Territory, op. cit.,* 111 (West gives the year, erroneously, as "1903").

Chapter 17

1. Muskogee, I.T. dispatch, January 9, *Daily Oklahoman,* January 10, 1905.

2. Muskogee, I.T. dispatch, January 16, *Daily Oklahoman,* January 17, 1905.

3. *Tulsa Daily Democrat,* March 23, 1905.

4. Muskogee, I.T. dispatch, April 4, *Oklahoma State Capital,* April 5, 1905; Muskogee, I.T. dispatch, April 8, *Daily Oklahoman,* April 9, 1905.

5. Benedict, *op. cit.,* 281-282.

6. Muskogee, I.T. dispatch, April 5, *Oklahoma State Capital,* April 6, 1905.

7. *Daily Oklahoman,* November 5, 7, and 19, 1904.

8. Tulsa, I.T. dispatch, December 12, *Daily Oklahoman,* December 13, 1904.

9. Muskogee *Times-Democrat,* August 23, 1905.

10. Muskogee, I.T. dispatch, August 14, *Oklahoma State Capital,* August 15, 1905.

11. Muskogee *Times-Democrat,* October 5, 1905.

Chapter 18

1. *Tulsa Daily Democrat,* June 12, 1905.

2. *Ibid.,* October 25, 1905; Ronald L. Trekell, *History of the Tulsa Police Department, 1882-1990* (privately printed, Tulsa, Oklahoma, 1989), 22-28.

3. *Tulsa Daily Democrat,* October 25 and November 4 and 7, 1905.

4. Trekell, *op. cit.,* 28.

5. *Tulsa Daily Democrat,* October 21, 1905.

6. *Ibid.,* October 2, 1905.

7. *Ibid.*

8. *Ibid.,* November 4, 1905.

9. *Ibid.,* November 3 and 4, 1905.

10. *Ibid.,* November 4, 1905

11. *Ibid.,* November 7, 1905.

12. Trekell, *op. cit.,* 28.

13. *Tulsa Daily Democrat,* November 4, 1905.

14. *Ibid.,* November 11, 1905.

Chapter 19

1. *Tulsa Daily Democrat,* November 18, 1905.

2. Muskogee, I.T. dispatch, December 8, *Tulsa Daily World,* December 9, 1905.

3. *Tulsa Daily Democrat,* December 27, 1905.

4. *Ibid.,* January 31, 1906.

5. *Ibid.*

6. *Ibid.,* March 2, 1906.

7. Muskogee, I.T. dispatch, January 29, *Tulsa Daily Democrat,* January 29, 1906; *Oklahoma State Capital,* January 30, 1906.

8. *Ibid.*

9. Eufaula *Indian Journal,* February 9, 1906; Muskogee *Times-Democrat,* February 9, 1906.

10. Judge Williams, *op. cit.,* 135; Benedict, *op. cit.,* 394; Johnson, compiler, *op. cit.,* 163.

11. Muskogee, I.T. dispatch, February 3, *Oklahoma State Capital,* February 3, 1906.

12. Muskogee *Times-Democrat,* October 4, 1909.

13. Muskogee, I.T. dispatch, February 22, *Oklahoma State Capital,* February 23, 1906.

14. Muskogee, I.T. dispatch, March 19, *Oklahoma State Capital,* March 20, 1906.

15. *Ibid.*

16. Muskogee, I.T. dispatch, March 29, *Daily Oklahoman,* March 30, 1906; Muskogee, I.T. dispatch, March 30, *Oklahoma State Capital,* March 31, 1906.

17. Muskogee, I.T. dispatch, May 23, *Daily Oklahoman,* May 24, 1906; *Tulsa Daily Democrat,* May 24, 1906.

18. *Ibid.*

19. Muskogee, I.T. dispatch, May 26, *Tulsa Daily Democrat,* May 26, 1906.

20. Muskogee, I.T. dispatch, May 28, *Tulsa Daily Democrat,* May 28, 1906.

Chapter 20

1. *Tulsa Daily Democrat,* June 18, 1906.

2. Baron Creager, "Toughest Man in the Territory," *Tulsa Daily World,* June 22, 1969.

3. *Tulsa Daily Democrat,* August 25 and 27, 1906.

4. *Ibid.*

5. *Ibid.*

6. Eufaula, I.T. dispatch, September 22, *Daily Oklahoman,* September 23, 1906; Eufaula, I.T. dispatch, September 24, *Tulsa Daily Democrat,* September 24, 1906; Creager, *op. cit.*

7. Muskogee, I.T. dispatch, November 19, *Oklahoma State Capital,* November 20, 1906; Muskogee, I.T. dispatch, November 20, *Tulsa Daily Democrat,* November 20, 1906.

8. Wagoner, I.T. dispatch, December 17, *Daily Oklahoma,* December 18, 1906.

9. Muskogee, I.T. dispatch, January 16, *Tulsa Daily Democrat,* January 16, 1907.

10. *Tulsa Daily Democrat,* March 4, 1907.

11. *Daily Oklahoman,* January 19, 1907.

Chapter 21

1. Muskogee, I.T. dispatch, March 21, *Oklahoma State Capital,* March 22, 1907.

2. Wewoka, I.T. dispatch, March 26, *Oklahoma State Capital,* March 27, 1907.

3. Okmulgee, I.T. dispatch, March 26, *Daily Oklahoman,* March 27, 1907.

4. Details of the fight appear in Muskogee, I.T. dispatch, March 26, *Daily Oklahoman,* March 27, 1907; *Oklahoma State Capital,* March 27 and 29, 1907; *Muskogee Phoenix,* March 26, 1922; Col. Douglas, *op. cit.*

Summarized in Foreman, *op. cit.,* 140; West, *Persons and Places in Indian Territory, op. cit.,* 132, and *Outlaws and Peace Officers of Indian Territory, op. cit.,* 112-113; Starr and Hill, *op. cit.,* 86-88.

5. Col. Douglas, *op. cit.*

6. *Ibid.*

7. Muskogee, I.T. dispatch, March 26, *Daily Oklahoman,* March 27, 1907; *Oklahoma State Capital,* March 29, 1907.

8. Muskogee, I.T. dispatch, April 8, *Daily Oklahoman,* April 9, 1907.

Chapter 22

1. Porum, I.T. dispatch, July 5, *Daily Oklahoman,* July 6, 1907.

2. Muskogee, I.T. dispatch, July 10, *Oklahoma State Capital,* July 11, 1907.

3. *Ibid.*

4. Muskogee, I.T. dispatch, July 11, *Daily Oklahoman,* July 12, 1907.

5. *Ibid.*

6. Muskogee, I.T. dispatch, July 18, *Daily Oklahoman,* July 19, 1907; *Oklahoma State Capital,* July 20, 1907.

7. Muskogee, I.T. dispatch, March 18, *Oklahoma State Capital,* March 19, 1907.

8. *Oklahoma State Capital,* November 15, 1907.

Chapter 23

1. "'Bud' Ledbetter, Pioneer Officer," *Muskogee Phoenix,* July 9, 1937.

2. "Bud Ledbetter, Famous Early Bandit Fighter," *Daily Oklahoman,* November 12, 1922.

3. Session Laws of 1907-1908, First Legislative Assembly of the State of Oklahoma, pp. 183-185.

4. Muskogee *Times-Democrat,* March 6, 1908.

5. *Ibid.,* March 20, 1908.

6. "Noted Outlaw Catcher," *Oklahoma State Capital,* March 29, 1908.

7. LaVere Shoenfelt Anderson, " 'Uncle Bud' Ledbetter, Territory Terror, Not Yet Through," *Tulsa Daily World,* May 21, 1933; " 'Bud' Ledbetter, Pioneer Officer," *op. cit.*

Also West, *Persons and Places in Indian Territory, op. cit.,* 133, and *Outlaws and Peace Officers of Indian Territory, op. cit.,* 114.

8. Muskogee *Times-Democrat,* June 29, 1908.

9. *State ex rel. West, Atty. Gen., v. Ledbetter,* No. 175, 22 Oklahoma Reports 251.

10. *State ex rel. Kline v. Bridges, Mayor,* No. 107, 20 Oklahoma Reports 533.

11. *State ex rel. West, Atty. Gen., v. Ledbetter,* No. 175, op. cit.

12. *Ledbetter v. King, Judge,* No. 1710, 26 Oklahoma Reports 469; *Oklahoma State Capital,* December 9, 1910.

Chapter 24

1. Muskogee dispatch, October 22, *Daily Oklahoman,* October 23, 1911.

2. Muskogee dispatch, February 14, *Daily Oklahoman,* February 15 1912.

3. Muskogee dispatch, February 17, *Daily Oklahoman,* February 18, 1912.

4. "Marshal Ordered to Enforce Laws," *Daily Oklahoman,* March 5, 1912; "U.S. Prohibition Is Some Serious," *Daily Oklahoman,* March 13, 1912.

5. Muskogee *Times-Democrat,* December 27, 1912.

6. Muskogee dispatch, December 24, *Tulsa Daily Democrat,* December 24, 1914.

7. Muskogee *Times-Democrat,* December 5, 1914.

8. *Muskogee Phoenix,* January 1, 1915.

9. Muskogee *Times Democrat,* June 29, 1915.

Chapter 25

1. "Bud Ledbetter, Famous Early Bandit Fighter," *op. cit.*; " 'Bud' Ledbetter, Pioneer Officer," *op. cit.*

Also Starr and Hill, *op. cit.,* 90; West, *Persons and Places in Indian Territory, op. cit.,* 135, and *Outlaws and Peace Officers of Indian Territory, op. cit.,* 115.

2. "Bud Ledbetter, Famous Early Bandit Fighter, Not Too Old To Be Sheriff, Voters Think," *Daily Oklahoman,* November 12, 1922; Benedict, *op. cit.,* 460, 463.

3 " 'Bud' Ledbetter, Pioneer Officer," *op. cit.*; West, *Persons and Places in Indian Territory, op. cit.,* 135, and *Outlaws and Peace Officers of Indian Territory, op. cit.,* 115.

4. McKennon, "On the Side of the Law," *op. cit.*; West, *Persons and Places in Indian Territory, op. cit.,* 140, and *Outlaws and Peace Officers of Indian Territory, op. cit.,* 118.

5. Starr and Hill, *op. cit.*, 91.

6. Benedict, *op. cit.*, 463; " 'Bud' Ledbetter, Pioneer Officer," *op. cit.*; West, *Persons and Places in Indian Territory, op. cit.*, 137, and *Outlaws and Peace Officers of Indian Territory, op. cit.*, 116; Starr and Hill, *op. cit.*, 90.

7. LaVere Shoenfelt Anderson, *op. cit.*

8. J. Kendall M'Claren, " 'Uncle Bud' Passes 82 Quietly on Farm," *Muskogee Phoenix*, December 16, 1934; " 'Bud' Ledbetter, Pioneer Officer," *op. cit.*

9. *Muskogee Phoenix*, July 9, 1937; *Tulsa Daily World*, July 9, 1937; *Tulsa Tribune*, July 9, 1937.

10. *Muskogee Phoenix*, July 11, 1937.

Bibliography

Documents

Buz Luckey v. United States, 163 U.S. 162, 16 Supreme Court Reporter 1203.
Dyer v. United States, 164 U.S. 704, 17 Supreme Court Reporter 993.
In re Jennings, 118 Federal Reporter 479.
Jennings v. United States, Indian Territory Reports: Cases Determined in the United States Court of Appeals for the Indian Territory, Vol. II.
Ledbetter v. King, Judge, No. 1710, 26 Oklahoma Reports 469.
Ltr. Carl Fink (nephew of Deputy U.S. Marshal Ed Fink) to Glenn Shirley, May 8, 1961.
Session Laws of 1907-1908, First Legislative Assembly of the State of Oklahoma.
State ex. rel. Kline v. Bridges, Mayor, No.107, 20 Oklahoma Reports 533.
State ex. rel. West, Atty. Gen., v. Ledbetter, No. 175, 22 Oklahoma Reports 533.
U.S. Statutes at Large, 50th Congress, Session II, Vol. 25, chap. 333 (Act of March 1, 1889).
U.S. Statutes at Large, 51st Congress, Session I, Vol. 26, chap. 182 (Act of May 2, 1890).
U.S. Statutes at Large, 53rd Congress, Session III, Vol. 28, chap. 145 (Act of March 1, 1895).
U.S. Statutes at Large, 55th Congress, Session II, Vol. 30, chap. 3 (Act of June 7, 1897).
U.S. Statutes at Large, 55th Congress, Session II, Vol. 30, chap. 517 (Act of June 28, 1898—Curtis Bill).
33 U.S. Statutes at Large 245.
33 U.S. Statutes at Large 573.

Newspapers

Ardmore *State Herald,* November 22, 1894, August 22, 1895.

Daily Oklahoman, November 15, 1894; June 20, 1894; June 3, 1898; February 16-18, 1899; May 18, 1899; August 5, 1899; April 3, 1902; August 24, 27, 1902; September 3, 1902; November 13, 1902; June 20, 1903; January 12, 1904; May 27, 1904; July 5, 6, 8, 1904; November 5, 7, 19, 29, 1904; December 4, 6, 13, 1904; January 10, 17, 1905; April 9, 1905; March 30, 1906; May 24, 1906; September 23, 1906; December 18, 1906; January 19, 1907; March 27, 1907; April 9, 1907; July 6, 12, 19, 1907; October 23, 1911; February 15, 18, 1912;

Eufaula *Indian Journal,* December 9, 1904; December 1, 1905; February 9, 1906.

Eufaula Republican, August 16, 1912.

Fort Smith *Elevator,* April 17, 1891; August 30, 1895; January 31, 1896; October 16, 1896.

Guthrie Daily Leader, December 8, 1897.

Johnson County (Arkansas) *Herald,* March 9 through June 29, 1883; June 19, 1903.

Muskogee Phoenix, November 21, 1894; August 8, 15, 29, 1895; September 13, 19, 26, 1895; December 9, 30, 1897; February 3, 10, 24, 1898; March 10, 1898; April 14, 28, 1898; May 5, 12, 19, 26, 1898; June 2, 9, 30, 1898; July 7, 1898; October 6, 13, 1898; August 21, 1902; January 1, 1915; March 26, 1922; July 9, 11, 1937.

Muskogee *Times-Democrat,* August 23, 1905; October 5, 1905; February 9, 1906; March 6, 20, 1908; June 29, 1908; October 4, 1909; December 27, 1912; December 5, 1914; June 29, 1915.

Oklahoma Daily Times-Journal, August 24, 1895.

Oklahoma State Capital, August 9, 1895; October 17, 1895; September 1, 1896; December 8, 1897; February 16-18, 1899; January 27, 1901; February 8, 1901; May 6, 7, 1903; May 3, 20, 1904; April 5, 6, 1905; August 15, 1905; January 30, 1906; February 3, 23, 1906; March 20, 31, 1906; November 20, 1906; March 19, 22, 27, 29, 1907; July 11, 20, 1907; November 15, 1907; December 9, 1910.

Stillwater Gazette, November 26, 1903.

Tulsa Daily Democrat, December 26, 1904; March 23, 1905; June 12, 1905; October 25, 1905; November 3, 4, 7, 11, 18, 1905; December 27, 1905; January 29, 31, 1906; March 2, 1906; May 24, 26, 28, 1906; June 18, 1906; August 25, 27, 1906; September 24, 1906; January 16, 1907; March 4, 1907; December 24, 1914.

Tulsa Daily World, December 9, 1905; December 15, 1936; July 9, 1937.

Tulsa Tribune, July 9, 1937.

Vinita *Indian Chieftain,* March 7, 1889; July 26, 1894; November 14, 15, 1894; December 27, 1894; August 8, 29, 1895; September 26, 1895; March 12, 1896; October 15, 1896; December 3, 1896; December 30, 1897; April 4, 1901; November 14, 1901.

Interviews

In *Indian Pioneer History,* Oklahoma Historical Society, Archives and Manuscript Division, Volumes 1-112.
Adams, Harry H. Vol. 99, 33-43.
Jones, William Frank. Vol. 6, 21-45.
Lewis, S. R. Vol. 78, 258-263.
Reed, Nathaniel (Texas Jack). Vol. 41, 307-313.
Ridenhour, H. E. Vol. 113, 402-410.
Sunday, Ed. Vol. 46, 61-92.

Books

Benedict, John D. *Muskogee and Northeastern Oklahoma.* Vol. II. Chicago: S. J. Clarke Publishing Company, 1922.

Campbell, O. B. *Vinita, I.T. The Story of a Frontier Town of the Cherokee Nation, 1871-1907.* Oklahoma City: Oklahoma Publishing Company, 1969.

Foreman, Grant. *Muskogee, The Biography of an Oklahoma Town.* Norman: University of Oklahoma Press, 1943.

Gittinger, Roy. *The Formation of the State of Oklahoma, 1803-1906.* Berkeley: University of California Press, 1917.

Harman, S. W. *Hell on the Border: He Hanged Eighty-Eight Men.* Fort Smith, AR: The Phoenix Publishing Company, 1898.

History of Northwest Arkansas. History of Benton, Washington, Carroll, Madison, Crawford, Franklin and Sebastian Counties. Chicago: Goodspeed Publishing Company, 1889.

Jennings, Al and Will Irwin. *Beating Back.* New York: The Munson Book Company, Toronto — D. Appleton and Company, 1914.

Johnson, Roy M. (compiler). *Oklahoma History, South of the Canadian.* Vol. I. Chicago: The S. J. Clarke Publishing Company, 1925.

Jones, William Frank. *The Experiences of a Deputy U.S. Marshal of the Indian Territory.* Tulsa, OK: privately printed, 1937.

McKennon, C. H. *Iron Men: A Saga of the Deputy United States Marshals Who Rode the Indian Territory.* Garden City, NY: Doubleday and Company, 1967.

Mooney, Charles W. *Localized History of Pottawatomie County, Oklahoma to 1907.* Midwest City, OK: privately printed, 1971.

Reed, Nathaniel. *The Life of Texas Jack: Eight Years a Criminal, 41 Years Trusting in God.* Tulsa, OK: By Himself, 1936.

Shirley, Glenn. *West of Hell's Fringe: Crime, Criminals and the Federal Peace Officer in Oklahoma Territory, 1889-1907.* Norman: University of Oklahoma Press, 1978.

Stansbery, Lon. R. *The Passing of the 3-D Ranch.* Tulsa, OK: privately printed, 1930.

Starr, Helen, and O. E. Hill. *Footprints in the Indian Nation.* Muskogee, OK: Hoffman Printing Company, Inc., 1974.

Thomas, David Y. (editor). *Arkansas and Its People.* Vol. II. New York: American Historical Society, 1930.

Trekell, Ronald L. *History of the Tulsa Police Department, 1882-1990*. Tulsa, OK: privately printed, 1989.

West, C. W. "Dub." *Outlaws and Peace Officers of Indian Territory*. Muskogee, OK: Muskogee Printing Company, 1987.

———. *Persons and Places in Indian Territory*. Muskogee, OK: Muskogee Publishing Company, 1974.

Articles

Adams, Harry H. "The Brush Court in Indian Territory," *Chronicles of Oklahoma*, Vol. XLVI, No. 2, Summer 1968.

Anderson, LaVere Shoenfelt. " 'Uncle Bud' Ledbetter, Territory Terror, Not Yet Through," *Tulsa Daily World*, May 21, 1933.

"Bud Ledbetter, Famous Early Bandit Fighter, Not Too Old To Be Sheriff, Voters Think," *Daily Oklahoman*, November 12, 1922.

" 'Bud' Ledbetter, Pioneer Officer," *Muskogee Phoenix*, July 9, 1937.

Clark, J. Stanley. "The Career of John R. Thomas," *Chronicles of Oklahoma*, Vol. LII, No. 2, Summer 1974.

Creager, Baron. "Toughest Man in the Territory," *Tulsa Daily World*, June 22, 1969.

Douglas, Col. Clarence B. "Bud Ledbetter's One-Man Race Riot," *Daily Oklahoman*, April 5, 1936.

Foreman, Grant. "Oklahoma's First Court," *Chronicles of Oklahoma*, Vol. XIII, No. 4, December 1935.

Gill, Jr., Joseph A. "Judge Joseph Albert Gill, 1854-1933," *Chronicles of Oklahoma*, Vol. XII, No. 3, September 1934.

Gold, Freda. " 'Best' Deputy Marshal Will Begin 50th Year," *Tulsa Daily World*, June 29, 1952.

———. "Marshal to Give Up Badge After 50 Years of Service," *Tulsa Daily World*, October 24, 1952.

Hoge, Bill. "Oologah Oozings," *Tulsa Sunday World Magazine*. August 19, 1956.

"How the Creek Indians Lost Millions of Dollars: Civil War Recruits Still Apparent—Indians Once Owned Slaves Who Gobbled Up the Best of Lands," Stillwater *Advance-Democrat*, May 5, 1904.

"The Jennings Jerked," *Muskogee Phoenix*, December 9, 1897.

Larson, E. Dixon and Al Ritter. "Leo E. Bennett, Indian Territory Pioneer and Lawman," *Oklahoma State Trooper*, Spring 1995.

"Marshal Ordered to Enforce Laws," *Daily Oklahoman*, March 5, 1912.

Martin, Benjamin. "Charles W. Raymond, 1858-1939," *Chronicles of Oklahoma*, Vol. XVII, No. 2, September 1939.

Meserve, John Bartlett. "From Parker to Poe," *Chronicles of Oklahoma*, Vol. XVI, No. 1, March 1938.

M'Claren, J. Kendall, " 'Uncle Bud' Passes 82 Quietly on Farm," *Muskogee Phoenix*, December 16, 1934.

McKennon, C. H. "Oklahoma's Long-Time Marshal," *The West*, Vol. 10, No. 6, May 1969.

———. "On the Side of the Law," *Tulsa Daily World*, November 5, 1961.

———. "There Was A Stillness, A Still and Lawmen," *Tulsa Daily World*, August 25, 1968.

———. "When Marshals and Outlaws Shot It Out," *Tulsa Daily World*, January 15, 1961.

Myers, Olevia E. "Two Sides of the Green Boys," *Old West*, Vol. 10, No. 4, Summer 1974.

"Noted Outlaw Catcher," *Oklahoma State Capital*, March 29, 1908.

"Oklahoma 'Six-Gun' Legends," *Tulsa Tribune*, July 9, 1937.

Rand, Jerry. "Samuel Morton Rutherford," *Chronicles of Oklahoma*, Vol. XXX, No. 2, Summer 1952.

Shirley, Glenn. "The Bungled Job at Blackstone Switch," *True West*, Vol 13, No. 2, May-June 1966.

Stansbery, Lon R. "Bud Ledbetter, Scourge of Criminals. Veteran Officer Relentless in Pursuit," *Tulsa Daily World*, January 24, 1937.

———. "Bud Ledbetter, Pioneer G-Man of the West," *Tulsa Daily World*, May 21, 1937.

"U.S. Prohibition Is Some Serious," *Daily Oklahoman*, March 13, 1912.

Underhill, Lonnie E. and Daniel F. Littlefield. "James F. Ledbetter, Frontier Lawman," *Red River Valley Historical Review*, Vol. I, No. 4, Winter 1974.

"Vinita Schedules Centennial Party," *Tulsa Daily World*, July 31, 1971.

Williams, Judge R. L. "The Judicial History of Oklahoma" (Proceedings of the Fifth Annual Meeting of the Oklahoma Bar Association, Oklahoma City, December 21-22, 1911).

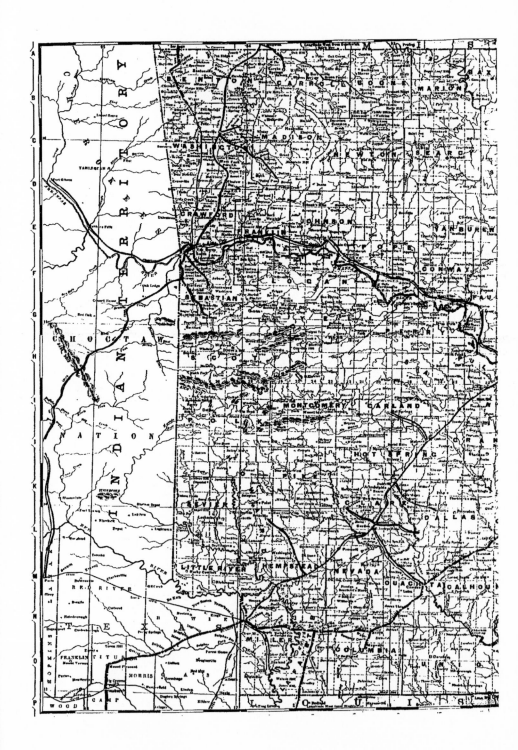

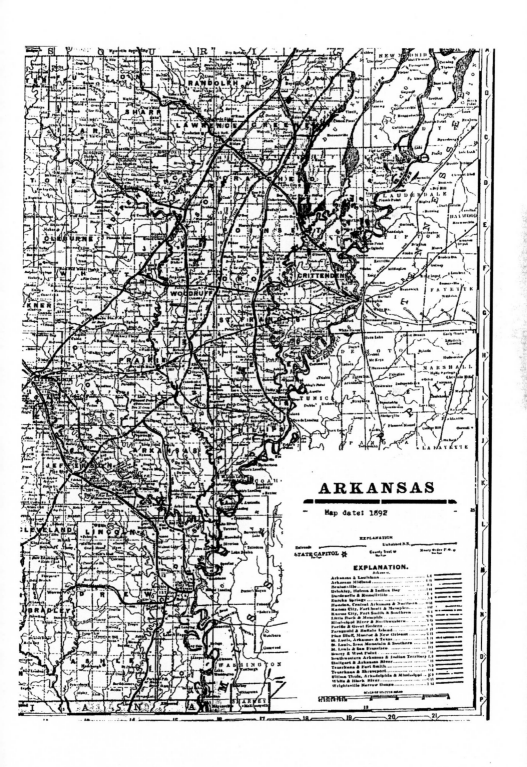

ARKANSAS

— Map date: 1892 —

EXPLANATION

Railroads   Unfinished R.R.

STATE CAPITOL   County Seat   Money Order P. O.

EXPLANATION.

Arkansas.

Arkansas & Louisiana	L 6
Arkansas Midland	R 5
Bentonville	A 6
Brinkley, Helena & Indian Bay	I 16
Dardanelle & Russellville	E 8
Eureka Springs	A 6
Houston, Central Arkansas & Northern	I 17
Kansas City, Fort Scott & Memphis	H 18
Kansas City, Fort Smith & Southern	H 8
Little Rock & Memphis	G 12
Mississippi River & Southwestern	C 9
Pacific & Great Eastern	C 5
Paragould & Buffalo Island	C 13
Pine Bluff, Monroe & New Orleans	I 15
St. Louis, Arkansas & Texas	I 11
St. Louis, Iron Mountain & Southern	B 5
St. Louis & San Francisco	B 5
Searcy & West Point	H 11
Southwestern Arkansas & Indian Territory	L 9
Stuttgart & Arkansas River	I 13
Texarkana & Fort Smith	H 8
Texarkana & Shreveport	O 8
Ultima Thule, Arkadelphia & Mississippi	K 9
White & Black River	G 11
Wrightsville Narrow Gauge	L 12

SCALE OF STATUTE MILES

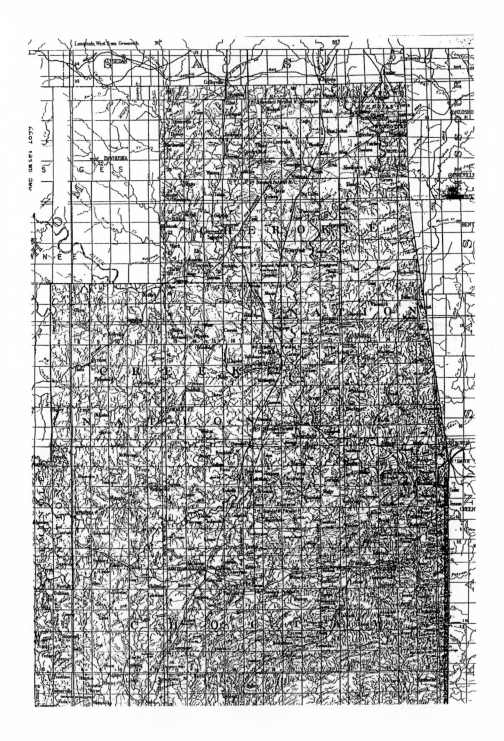

Index

[Note: Cities listed as being in Oklahoma in this index were formerly part of Indian Territory or Oklahoma Territory.]